VISIONS of PEACE

VISIONS of PEACE

Compiled and Edited
by SHIRLEY J. HECKMAN

Friendship Press, New York

Friendship Press, New York

Library of Congress in Publication Data
Visions of peace.
1. Peace—addresses, essays, lectures. 2. Just war doctrine—addresses, essays,
lectures. 3. Peace—study and teaching—addresses, essay, lectures.
I. Heckman, Shirley J., 1928–
JX1952.V53 1983 327.1'72 83-16522
ISBN 0-377-00140-6

ISBN 0-377-00140-6

Editorial Offices: 475 Riverside Drive, Room 772, New York, N.Y. 10115
Distribution Offices: P.O. Box 37844, Cincinnati, OH 45237
Copyright © 1984 Friendship Press, Inc.
Printed in the United States of America

CONTENTS

LIST OF POETRY AND MUSIC

PREFACE

As I write this, it is a sunny Saturday morning in June in Elgin, Illinois. The rain has finally quit. This morning, I rode my bicycle from home to the office, about five miles. My stomach is full. I, my husband, our sons, daughters and grandchildren are all healthy. When we turn on the faucet, clean water is available. I chose the clothes I am wearing today from among several possibilities. Our house is warm and comfortable in the winter; cool and comfortable in the summer. I have friends and colleagues who support and nurture me. My life is full of meaning, satisfaction and love. I have freedom to make many decisions about my life.

My vision of peace in the world is a very simple one. I want everyone on earth to have what I have. All people ought to have plenty of food, comfortable living quarters, clean water, love, meaning and freedom in their lives. That must be possible. All people everywhere should have some measure of control over their lives. They should have the freedom to ride a bicycle, if they want to do so.

You and I know, though, that my situation and probably your similar one are unusual in the world. I assume that your situation is similar to mine because you have the time and energy to devote to reading a book like this one. Most people in the world have to struggle for enough to eat. They have to work to get water and then it is often unclean. They have to decide whether they or their children will get what little food is available to them. They are at the mercy of their hunger and poverty. They have no escape from that grind which life is for them. The time and energy of their lives is consumed by their efforts to simply stay alive.

My vision for peace, though, is not unlike that of several passages of the Old Testament. Among them are 1 Kings 4:25, Micah 4:4, Isaiah 36:16 and Zachariah 3:10. It is a vision of sitting under a vine and a fig tree at peace and unafraid. In Micah, a needed community dimension is added to this vision with the prophesy that people will invite their neighbors to sit with them under their vines and fig trees.

To state such a vision is simple. But, we can not honestly tell ourselves that we are at peace or that we live unafraid. War and preparation for war are very much a part of our lives, though many of us are comfortably insulated from the pain that war and preparation for war inflict on others. We live with the numbing fear that in an instant, and without any direct action by us as individuals, our world can be destroyed or become a living hell for the survivors of nuclear explosions. And the results are the same whether the explosions are intentional or accidental.

War and preparation for war are blocks to my vision, to all visions, of peace. The issues surrounding the possibility of peace in our time are multi-faceted. The world is complex. Those in power are entrenched in current ideas about the best ways of maintaining control. Figuring out how to bring such a vision of peace to reality is difficult.

This book is your invitation to struggle both with forming a vision of peace and determining a course of action to bring that vision to reality. Included in this resource are varieties of visions. These are the opinions of the authors of the articles, rather than being official statements of the National Council of Churches of Christ or of any one denomination. It is hoped that those who read and study this material will pay careful attention to the different ideas, thinking through the visions and their worth.

Views of people of faith on war and peace issues range from those who are certain that reaching desirable ends justifies violent means to those who hold with equal conviction the belief that war is never acceptable and to threaten people with violence is equally unacceptable. Included in this book are only a few of the possible visions. The reasons for including each vision is stated in the introductory material of each article.

The book is in two parts. Part One centers on stating visions of peace from several perspectives. Illustrations of action toward making such visions a reality are given in Part Two.

A variety of visions are presented in Part One. The first section is my introduction. It deals with dreams and visions and with my statement of appropriate qualities for such visions. Also included are visions of peace from religious perspectives including statements from a Christian from the United States, a Jew, a Buddhist and a Christian from the U.S.S.R.

A theologian who teaches in both the United States and Germany then compares two visions of peace from the Bible and tells her perceptions of their application today. Next, a model of peacekeeping through a new form of security and a vision of possible steps toward general and complete disarmament are shared.

Other visions are seen, too. A former conscientious objector gives his rationale for just war. Then, violent revolution is described as necessary by two Christians, one of Zambia and the other of Nicaragua.

Part Two provides models for peace action. Guidelines for peace education are related to developmental understandings of children and youth. Vignettes give glimpses of disarmament activity in Canada. The protests of youth of East Germany are described. Tolstoy's letter of 1899 to a young man facing the draft seems surprisingly current. Short pieces tell about a farmer in Ohio and an older woman in California. A short history of an organization working for peace is given as an illustration of hundreds of similar groups.

INTRODUCTION: ABOUT DREAMS AND VISIONS

by Shirley Heckman

In the preface, this writer's vision was stated in biblical terms as "each one neath a vine and fig tree." Those words are used in music along with the words which state the theme of this study "swords into plowshares." It can be sung as a round.

Vine and Fig Tree

Shalom Altma

And ev-'ry one 'neath a vine and fig tree, Shall live in

peace and un - a - fraid. And ev-'ry fraid.

And in -to plough - shares turn their swords,

na - tions shall learn war no more. war no more.

Isaiah 4:25. Micah 4:3-4
* Second Group singing Ⓑ music may enter at * on second repeat of Ⓐ

In this introduction, my understandings about dreams and visions provide another way of expressing what my vision of peace is. In it, I state that:

—Everyone has dreams.

—Some visions are false and misleading.

— The image of people under vines and fig trees includes characteristics of world-changing visions. It is universal. It is future oriented. It requires commitment.

Dreaming and creating visions are part of everyday life. People do it all the time. The universality of dreaming can be seen in the words of music in recent years.

"You've got to have a dream,
If you don't have a dream,
How are you going to have a dream come true?"

Or that song from the musical about a dreamer, "The Man of LaMancha"

"To dream the impossible dream,
To right the unrightable wrong,..."

T. E. Lawrence wrote:

"All persons dream but not equally. Those who dream by night in the dusty recesses of their minds wake up in the day to find that it's vanity.... But the dreamers of the day are dangerous humans for they act out their dreams with open eyes to make them possible."

Deliberate dreaming, the dreaming of the day, has been called by a variety of names. Some call them visions. Others might label them long-range planning. For some, prayer is the name given this activity of "dangerous humans." The intentional passion in the statement that "prayer is the soul's sincere desire" is present in the deliberate dreaming of the daytime.

When people dream and create visions, they are trying to express the nearly inexpressible. They use poetry, symbols, songs, parables and stories to carry the messages of their dreams and visions. Science fiction and fantasy are vehicles for dreams reaching beyond some imaginations.

The scripture contains many references to dreams, dreamers, visions and prophets. Ezekiel, Daniel, Isaiah, the Josephs of both the Old and New Testaments, Mary, Herod and John on Patmos are only some of these biblical dreamers.

Dreams and visions provide motivation for the tasks that must be done. They give a starting point for planning what to do next and evaluating what has happened before. Abraham's vision sustained him as he and his people moved away from their home into a foreign land. Ruth's vision of solidarity with her mother-in-law led her into a new life. The Joseph of the Old Testament was both a dreamer and an interpreter of dreams. He learned in his later years to share his dreams in a way that was not as destructive as it had been in his youth. He learned how to use his dreams as a way of helping Egypt to plan a different way of living. Thus he provided food for hungry persons of many lands.

FALSE DREAMS

A song from the musical "Joseph and the Amazing Technicolor Dreamcoat" has these lines:

"Far, far away, someone was weeping,
But the world was sleeping.
Any dream will do...
The light is dimming and the dream is, too.
The world and I, we are still waiting,
Still hesitating.
Any dream will do."

It is not true that any dream will do. Some dreams have been and continue to be destructive. Hitler's vision of the Aryan master race is an extreme example. Sometimes dreams are only misleading or deluding.

Two warnings from Scripture:

"Ask rain from God in the season
of the spring rain,
from God who makes the storm clouds,
who gives people showers of rain and
to everyone the vegetation in the field;
for the teraphim (household gods) utter nonsense,
and diviners see lies,
the dreamers tell false dreams,
and give empty consolation.
Therefore the people wander about like sheep;
they are afflicted for want of a shepherd."
— Zechariah 10:1-2

"Do not listen to words of the prophets who prophesy
to you, filling you up with vain hopes;
they speak visions of their own minds,
not from the mouth of the Lord."
— Jeremiah 23:16

So how can persons know when their dreams and visions are false. One is simple denial and longing for that which is not. Other false dreams deal with either the past or the future without taking the present seriously. Some reduce the scope of the dreams and visions to be only for the dreamers, one small group of people, the dreamer's households or nation. Some false dreams miss the mark because they are dreamed in isolation away from other people. Some are shared in ways that others cannot comprehend.

Denial and wishing for that which is not. Some dreams are false because they are conditional. The clue to these misleading dreams is the language of "if only...then..." People do this in their personal lives with such statements as: "If only I had married a different person, then..." or, "If only we had a bigger house, more money...then we would be happy."

In their work worlds, individuals tell themselves: "If only I had the connections that she does, then I would be a success." "If only I had the job that he does, then I could make changes around here and be happy." "If only my job was more exciting, then I wouldn't waste time."

Internationally, North Americans tell themselves: "If only the rest of the world were like us, then we could have peace." "If only the United States can stay ahead of the U.S.S.R. in armaments, then we will be safe."

Denying reality creates this misleading base for visions. The marriage, the house, the money and the job and the world as they really are – all of these are gifts from God. False dreams keep dreamers from this important reality. Their current circumstances are gifts from God and must be the starting point for any change. This is not to say that the way things are is how they should stay. Rather, the way things are is the beginning point on the way to what they can become.

Dealing with only past or future. Some false dreams deal only with the past or only with the future without taking the present seriously. Those words from Joel that Peter used at Pentecost speak of the young seeing visions and the old dreaming dreams. (Joel 2:28, Acts 2:17). Misleading dreams do not deal with the present realistically or identify action in which to engage.

In a group, a young man shared his vision of what the church might be. His dream was vivid and intriguing.

When questioned about what might make his dream become a reality, he could not describe even one action that he could take. He was not ready to take any responsibility for seeing that his vision became a reality. His vision was of some dreamy future with no connection to his present action.

This writer's father was nearly 90 years old when I last visited him. He was clear about what was happening around him most of the time. His conversation, though, was about the glories of the past. He yearned for yesterdays long gone. His dreaming was only of the past.

The experience of the past will become part of dreams and visions. Dreams and visions, though, must enable people to live in the present as it is given to them. People need help in maintaining connection with the past, while anticipating the future, as they participate creatively in the present.

Reducing visions. Visions are also misleading when they are reduced in time, space or concept. If dreams are only for the ones who dream them, for their families, for their nation, or only for people like them, then they lead the dreamers astray. Some will say that world peace will come only when all people everywhere experience peace within themselves. Or they say that world peace will come when all the world decides that the United States or the Canadian or some other form of government is the right one. This kind of reduced vision is heard in these familiar words, "We ought to be stronger militaristically than the Russians because we are morally superior." The dreams and visions to which Christians are called are for the whole of God's created earth and for all the people of the world.

Dreaming in isolation. Dreams may turn out to be empty and powerless if they are shared in a way that cannot be understood. The style of the young Joseph in the Old Testament shows how this can happen. His dream-sharing puzzled his father and angered his brothers. Later in his life, he had learned how to share his dreams so that others could be part of bringing them to reality.

Sharing of one's vision with others allows people to move more effectively into the future. No one can be human alone. Dom Helder Camara, archbishop of Olinda and Recife, Brazil, said, "When we dream alone, it remains only a dream. When we dream together, it is not just a dream, it is the beginning of reality."

THE VISION OF THE GOSPEL

Christians are called to be creators with God of a world in which each one can live "'neath a vine and fig tree, at peace and unafraid." Visions of that reality are stated in Matthew 25. The writer of Isaiah 58 raises the unavoidable demands of social justice, compassion, love of neighbor and renewed identification with God. These same demands were stated by Jesus in the synagogue as reported in Luke 4.

The specifics of the situations were different in the times of the prophets and of Jesus than they are now. But pain, suffering, injustice and human need are still realities. The presence of "God with us" still happens when Christians participate with others in bringing relief to the hungry and justice to the oppressed.

That vision of what life could be when God's realm is

recognized on earth is the one Jesus as Messiah came to proclaim, to witness to, and to die for. It is that vision Christians are called upon to live. That is the context for world-changing dreams. To become realities, Christian dreams and visions must have the qualities of any world-changing dream. But they must also have the added dimensions which the Christian faith provides.

World-changing dreams are universal and particular. The world was changed when the vision of sailing around the world became reality. That happened in the particular action of a group of people actually leaving port. The God Christians serve is the continuing creator of all the universe who loves ALL the people of the earth equally. Jesus as the Christ is an example of that universal love. He manifested that universal love through meeting particular human needs in specific situations.

Christians, too, are called to demonstrate that universal love as they relate to specific people in particular circumstances. This may mean that they decide to change their ways of living. U.S. and Canadian Christians are part of a small proportion of the world's population which controls most of the world's goods. Therefore, they might demonstrate love by working with others toward more equitable distribution of those goods. Demonstrating love may mean going to prison for refusal to register for the draft if the draft is seen as contrary to that love.

World-changing dreams are global and comprehensive. As Karl Marx sat in a library in England, he had a dream of how working-class people could take some control over their own destinies. His dream became a reality with world-changing consequences. Patterns of politics, economics and culture were radically altered all over the earth.

The actions Christians take in local situations can be reflections of the world's problems. As they create structures that will provide food to the hungry in their neighborhoods, Christians are dealing with what is a global problem. The dreams Christians have and the plans they make must be those which deal with as many dimensions of a problem as possible. For instance, to be effective, action in the political arena must also take into account economic and cultural factors.

World-changing dreams are future-oriented. These dreams take into account the heritage of the past. They consider the reality of the present. They paint realistic pictures of the possibilities for the future. An example of this is the space program. Ideas about what could be were developed far in advance of the first launches. A picture of the future was created years before the trip to the moon actually happened. That trip literally changed the image humankind had of the earth. Now the earth's people know themselves to be riding on a mysteriously beautiful bluish ball floating in black space. Old dreams of nationalistic supremacy or local self-sufficiency seem inadequate in the light of that new image of the earth.

Rubem Alves, a theologian from South America, has said that Christians, and the world's people, must quit planting pumpkin seeds in order to have pie next season and begin planting dates in order that their children's children may have food.

World-changing dreams require commitment. The visions that will change the world are those which demand from the visionaries a willingness to risk their lives. Sometimes they require a willingness to give up one's individual preferences for corporate action.

Think, for instance, of how many people have been trained in the armed forces of the United States and Canada to work as units, even to the giving of their lives, if necessary. Through the years, thousands have died for dreams and visions. Some of these visions were of new countries free from domination. Others were visions that the land of the Indians or other indigenous peoples rightfully belonged to newcomers. Some people followed dreams of making the world safe for democracy, dreams of ridding the earth of the threat of fascism, and dreams of containing Communism in Vietnam and Korea. People were willing to risk and to lose their lives for such dreams. Some of these dreams and visions may now seem false.

For Christians, world-changing dreams are those which require commitment. Christians are called to give their whole lives, to risk dying, to expend their energies to bring to reality their visions.

One of the most famous dream speeches of recent times is that of Martin Luther King, Jr., in August 1963. Thousands have heard it. Hundreds have worked to bring that dream to reality and continue to do so.

King was willing to die for that dream. He did not just risk physical death but was able to pour out his life energies to bring that vision closer to reality. Inscribed on the plaque in Memphis where King was shot are the words from Genesis that his brothers said about Joseph: "Here comes the dreamer. Come now, let us kill him and we shall see what becomes of his dreams."

Science fiction provides images about time and space that can set creativity and energy free to work now for that which may come for future generations. The Dune trilogy by Frank Herbert is only one of many examples of such ideas in science fiction. To most who saw the desert on the planet Dune, it was a wasteland in which nobody but a few tough people could live. But Pardot Kynes, the planetologist, had a dream that one day the desert would bloom. His whole being, for all of his life, was aimed at bringing that dream to reality.

Others tried to block him in his work. He figured out ways to get around the restrictions placed on him. He taught his son and other children to be ecologically literate and very patient. He trained them to think and respond differently to their situation than others before them had.

When he was asked how long it would take for the transformation toward which he was working to take place, he answered that it would be from 300 to 500 years. He said that the thing would not come in the lifetime of any person now living, not in the lifetimes of their grandchildren three times removed, but it would come. Until then the work must continue: the digging, the building, the planting, the training of the children.

The dreams Christians have for peace on earth will never be completed—at least, not in the lifetime of any person now living. The vision of the earth as a humane habitation in which each one can "sit 'neath a vine and fig tree at peace and unafraid" has been with the world for thousands of years now.

I BELIEVE IN WONDER

(Can be sung to the tune: "I Have a Dream")
I have a dream, a song to sing
Releasing hope in everything.
If you see the wonder
Of this fragile sphere,
You can shape the future
Live beyond your fear.
I believe in wonder
Something new in everything I see.
I believe in wonder
And I know this world is right for me.
I've crossed the stream.
I have a dream.

I have a dream of what's to be
That all create our destiny
And the destination
Makes it worth the while
Pushing through the darkness
Still another mile.
I believe in wonder
Something new in everything I see.
I believe in wonder
And I know this world is right for me.
I've crossed the stream.
I have a dream.

I've crossed the stream.
I have a dream.

  Song used by permission of the Institute of Cultural Affairs, 4750 North Sheridan Road, Chicago, Illinois 60640.

PART ONE: VISIONS OF PEACE

CREATION AS THE THEATER OF GOD'S GLORY

by Arie R. Brouwer

This article is excerpts from a speech given by Arie R. Brouwer at a conference sponsored by The Churches' Center for Theology and Public Policy, "Toward A Theology of Peacemaking for the Nuclear Age," March 8-10, 1983, in Washington, D.C. In the speech, which was the keynote for that conference, he uses the image of creation being the theater of God's glory and presents a vision of peacemaking as an improvisational drama in that theater.

Brouwer cited two sources for the image. One of three sub-themes for the 1982 once-in-seven-years-meeting of the General Council of the World Alliance of Reformed Churches was, "The Theater of Glory and the Threatened Creation's Hope." The phrase "theater of glory" is lifted directly from the writing of John Calvin, who speaks of creation as the "Theatrum gloriae Dei."

Brouwer held pastorates in Michigan and New Jersey, was general secretary of the Reformed Church in America, and is now Deputy General Secretary for the World Council of Churches in Geneva. He was one of a group of U.S. church representatives who talked with church representatives from the Soviet Union in 1979 in Geneva, later in the United States, and again in the Soviet Union. He has served as chairman of the committee of the National Council of Churches of Christ which is in continued dialogue with the churches of the Soviet Union.

How is peacemaking related to God's action in history and creation, judgment and redemption, and enmity? A rereading of the Old Testament accounts of creation with all their pulsating drama enhanced my appreciation of the image.

Then, I rediscovered that Karl Barth had also used it as the theme of his eighth lecture in *Dogmatics in Outline.* He says that God "creates, sustains and rules" the world as the theater of God's glory. Come along then on a visit to the theater.

We find ourselves in a vast natural theater in the round—without walls. Life is everywhere. The earth puts forth vegetation, which in turn puts forth seed and fruit—both pleasant to the sight and good for food. The seas swarm with life, birds soar and sweep across the heavens, and the animals are paraded before Adam to be named.

The creation displays the Creator's holiness, power, and majesty; God's love, goodness, and bounty. God is made visible in the world. Creation is the theater of God's glory. In this theater, there is no distinction between audience and actor. The aim of everyone and everything is to celebrate life in the presence of God—rich, full and abundant.

That celebration of life is the glory both of the Creator and of the creation. God and Adam and Eve play the leading roles in a drama in which every living thing, and the earth itself, have a part. Creator and creation are not in conflict. The Creator is glorified in the fulfillment of the creation, and the creation is fulfilled in glorifying the Creator.

THE PEACEABLE NEW AGE OF GOD

Before the coming of the prophets, Israel had derived its identity primarily from its history. Its present was defined by its past. Israel walked through the world in the presence of the God of Abraham, Isaac, and Jacob, believing that as God had delivered the people in the past, so would they be delivered in the present. They were a people of the Exodus, an event reenacted annually in the great festival of the Passover.

The prophets looked the other way. The present, they said, is defined by the future rather than by the past. That future is consistent with God's saving work in the past, but new nevertheless. The important point, expressed in different degrees by various prophets, was that God would do "a new thing." God would intervene in history as distinctly and sharply in the future as in the past. There would be a new exodus, a new Zion, a new David, even a new covenant and a new creation.

This prophetic vision of history followed a pattern which may be described as discontinuous continuity. The actions of God were not erratic or out of character. They were true and trustworthy, but radically new nonetheless. Frequently, the prophets spoke of the great and "terrible day" in which God would make war on the foes of God and vanquish them forever. Beyond this great battle, *on the other side of God's action,* lay the new age of peace. This new age of peace was envisioned as the gift of one God, who is both Creator and Redeemer. Peace is bestowed not only upon the nations, who shall learn war no more (Isa. 2:4), but upon the whole creation. The leopard shall lie down with the kid (Isa. 11:6), and:

"They shall not hurt or destroy in all my holy mountain; for the earth shall be full of the knowledge of God as the waters cover the sea. (Isa. 11:9)

In salvation as in suffering, what Christians separate into history and nature, are inextricably bound together here and everywhere in the Hebrew Scriptures. The world which God is saving encompasses all of the nations and the whole of creation.

THE COSMIC CHRIST

The prophetic vision of salvation for Israel and the nations reaches its climax in the servant songs of Isaiah. The servant of God brings forth justice and truth to the nations (Isa. 42:1-4). In Isaiah 49:5-6, God says, "It is too light a thing that you should be my servant to raise up the tribes of Jacob and to restore the preserved of Israel; I will give you as a light to the nations, that my salvation may reach the end of the earth."

However, unclear the identity of this servant in the prophetic writings, the New Testament writers, with one voice, proclaimed the fulfillment of this prophecy in the person of Jesus of Nazareth. He is the servant of God, the Anointed in whom the rule of God is made manifest to the whole world.

This Christ is also the one through whom all things were created (John 1) and in whom God has purposed to unite all things (Eph. 1:10). Salvation is not only for the nations, it is cosmic in scope. This Christ has disarmed the principalities and powers which held humanity and all creation in bondage (Col. 1:15). In the bold word of Ephesians, Christ is the peace (Eph. 1:14) who unites Jew and Gentile and reconciles both to God, in one body, through the cross. That body, the church, is by no means the sole sphere of God's activity in Christ, but it is the privileged instrument of God to make known this "mystery hidden for ages in God, who created all things." (Eph. 3:9)

A NEW CREATION

The ministry of this cosmic Christ is nothing less than the renewal of creation, the renewal of all people and of all things. In 2 Corinthians 5:17, Paul sees a sign of this promise in the life of faith, saying that anyone who is in Christ is a new creation. This new creation, of course, waits for its fulfillment in the believers' resurrection, which is the *central testimony of the Christian faith to the enduring value of our human existence.*

What we, as Christians, confess concerning our own radical renewal in the resurrection of the body, may also be confessed of the creation as a whole. The form of this world is passing away (1 Corinthians 7:31), but the earth itself will be renewed. Consistent with the prophetic vision of a peaceable New Age of God, the new heaven and the new earth is also a work of discontinuous continuity. There is no hint here of the world renewing itself or of its being renewed by humankind. The new heaven and the new earth is the old world made new by the creative word of God.

We, at this conference, and our contemporaries have, of course, few, if any, illusions about bringing in the new world. We are threatened not by the illusion of continuity, but by the fear of total discontinuity. We live under the shadow of extinction which undermines hope. It destroys our will to preserve our inheritance and to develop a legacy for future generations.

THE NEW JERUSALEM

A powerful word of hope is found in John's vision of the new Jerusalem, of which he says, "And the kings of the earth shall bring their glory into it . . . they shall bring into it the glory and honor of the nations." (Rev. 21:24-26) This vision is testimony that history will be fulfilled in the heavenly community of the Sovereign God. The new Jerusalem comes down from God, but it receives the cultural treasures of history. We do not have any assurance that we can organize the world to insure peace

and justice. We do, however, have assurance that our small victories are in essence signs of God's New Age and that they shall endure. They are seeds sown in history which shall bring forth their fruit in the New Age.

This hope is not for us alone but for the world. In their ancient vision of the New Age of God, the prophets had long since announced that the rule of God encompassed not only Israel, but the nations as well. Even Nebuchadnezzar and Cyrus are pressed into the service of God. The Creator God of Israel is the God of the nations. In the new Jerusalem, God provides a tree of life whose leaves are for the healing of the nations.

GOD'S COVENANT – CREATION'S HOPE

Not the new Jerusalem only, but the whole of God's work in history, is the ground of our hope – hope which can dispel the apocalyptic aura which threatens to overwhelm us.

Our hope is grounded in the certain confidence that our God is a covenant God, who keeps the word given to us, binding us to God and God to us. So our salvation was given as a gift of grace and is now rooted in the righteousness of God. Our salvation rests in the confidence that the judge of all the earth shall indeed do right.

Our hope is built on the knowledge that God's covenant is a covenant of peace, truth, justice, reconciliation and harmony. Our hope provides an enduring pattern for our life vision, and for our daily work, in the face of conflicting scenarios and overwhelming odds.

Our hope encompasses the whole of creation, whose ground and goal is the covenant in which God seeks communion with humankind in a world of shalom.

PEACEMAKING AS IMPROVISATIONAL THEATER

Of course, there will be conflict on the way to the peaceable New Age of God. Sometimes the conflict will be personal, sometimes it will be structural. Sometimes the conflict will arise out of situations, but always there will be conflict. The essence of drama is conflict. Our part, moreover, is played in the middle of the drama, in the second act, where the conflict is being worked out.

In this drama of God's redemption and creation, our task as peacemakers – indeed our whole task of Christian mission – may well be thought of in terms of improvisational theater. Like all theater, improvisational theater has a plot which defines the action, with a beginning, an end, and a middle. But unlike other theater, it does not have a script.

The players are assigned roles, subject to some negotiation, which are then carefully defined in terms of identity (Who am I?), goal (What do I want?), and struggling (What's in my way?). The drama is created through the interaction of the players, in their roles, and within the plot. The unfolding action requires careful relating, attentive listening, and creative participation on the part of each member of the cast. *The play, like God's work in creation and history, is a creative act whose ground and goal is covenant.*

This inseparability of creation and covenant may serve as an antidote to both "quietism" and activism. Activists tend to forget that creation is a gift of God given for the purpose of fulfilling the covenant of communion between God and creation. "Quietists" tend to forget that the covenant of communion requires fulfillment through acts of creation and re-creation. If either covenant or creaion is minimized, the drama loses its focus and so does our witness.

Nor can one think long of peacemaking in terms of creation and covenant without reflecting on our failure to act ecumenically. The peace movement is itself called to be a sign of the working out of God's covenant purpose for creation. Our common action in a covenant community is, therefore, more than a matter of management or morals. It is a matter of theological integrity and of faithful witness. Our message is shalom—wholeness, reconciliation, unity. Our failure to form a covenant community which demonstrates such shalom weakens our witness and gives an uncertain sound to our message. It makes the play look shaky.

Seeing peacemaking as improvisational participation in the drama of covenant and creation can also help us to keep our work in perspective. We have already noted the importance of an understanding of the end time as a mixture of continuity and discontinuity. Such an understanding helps protect us against revolutionary romanticism and utopianism on the one hand and against authoritarianism and other forms of escapism on the other hand.

Beginnings are no less important than endings. Take, for example, the pronouncement of creation as "very good." Modern biblical scholarship has freed this description from the concept of perfection imposed upon it by scholasticism. The Hebrew expression, as we have already noted, means that creation was declared good for God's purpose—which is communion with the creation, especially with human creation. This understanding freed from perfectionism can help to free peacemakers from perfectionism and idealism, from substituting rhetoric for reality, from playing Act 2 as if it were Act 3. It can set peacemakers free to be practical politicians, to play out the conflict between the beginning and the end, in order to set out signs of a world which is suitable for God's purpose.

This knowledge of beginnings and this vision of the end are not for their own sakes. They are to help us to play our parts in the middle. An improvisational company which forgets where it began and loses sight of its goal, slips from creation into chaos and from hope into despair. The play falls apart.

Other implications, I leave to your own improvisation. My main point is that when we see our peacemaking work and witness as improvisational participation in

The peace movement is always in danger of being transfixed by the terrible and monstrous evil we confront. God's story of creation and redemption, in the theater of God's glory without a script, we are free to act in hope. We peacemakers who believe in God should, therefore, not base our appeal on the statistics of overkill or on the rhetoric of horror and extinction, both of which numb the mind and weaken the will. These must be named and confronted. But, we who believe in God should exercise our freedom to confront them in hope.

This hope is grounded in the certainty that this is God's world. God is renewing it. We are God's. The drama is God's. And, God invites us to play our part and to develop the drama as God leads us all toward shalom.

Used by permission of the Churches Center for Theology and Public Policy, Washington, D.C. Edited for this publication.

BELIEVE

(Can be sung to the tune: "The Sloop John B")

Chorus:
Believe that the time has come
This world's going to live as one
And people are ready now
To create a new way.
New spirit alive
New dream on the rise
One world together
Create the new day.

Everybody can see
A new way that it can be
But so many things just seem
to get in the way.
The chains that bind us are strong
The road to liberty long
Toward one world together
New earth, a new day.

Listen and you will hear
The future is coming clear
And everybody alive
has something to say.
Sharing a bit of the load
We're walking down the same road
Working together
New earth, a new day.

Song used by permission of the Institute of Cultural Affairs, 4750 North Sheridan Road, Chicago, Illinois 60640.

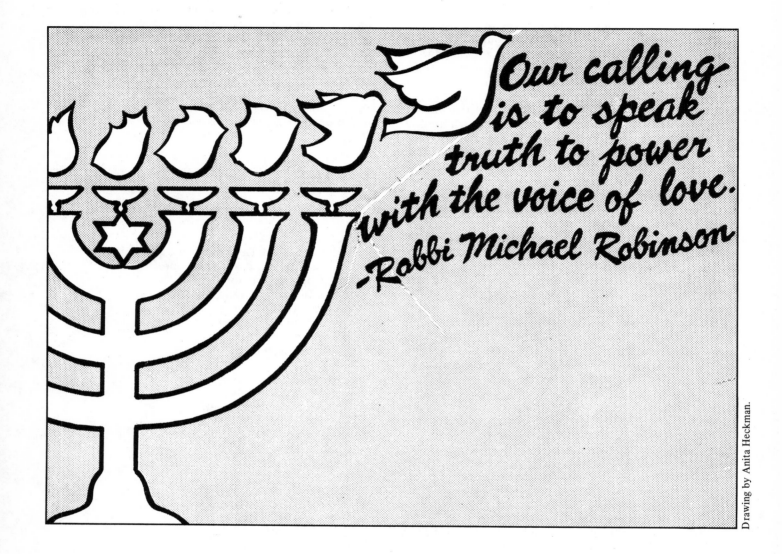

Our calling is to speak truth to power with the voice of love.
-Rabbi Michael Robinson

Drawing by Anita Heckman.

6

THE JEWISH COVENANT OF PEACE: POST-BIBLICAL PEACEMAKING & THE CALL TO FAITHFULNESS.

by Rabbi Michael Robinson

Rabbi Michael Robinson is National Vice-Chairman of the Fellowship of Reconciliation and a board member of the Union of American Hebrew Congregations. He lives in Croton-on-the-Hudson, N.Y., where he has served as spiritual leader of Temple Israel of Northern Westchester since 1960.

This article is an excerpt from a talk given by Rabbi Robinson on March 9, 1982, at the St. Paul's Methodist Church in San Jose while he and his wife were on a tour sponsored by the Fellowship of Reconciliation.

In it Rabbi Robinson makes a clear call for action toward peacemaking. He states our call as people of faith to be the basis for that action. He identifies two threads in the Bible. One is the story of the feisty people fighting their way through history. The other is the experience of mystical encounter with God. The biblical draft law is noted. He asks us to consider God's caring about all the children in the world not just those who agree with us. His orientation toward the future is evidence in his willingness to plant an apple tree even if the world were to be destroyed.

The big Madison Avenue advertising campaign that we used to see on billboards and subways in New York, showed a Chinese man, a black man and a Puerto Rican eating a sandwich. It said, "You don't have to be Jewish to love Levy's rye bread." I say, you don't have to be Jewish to be a member of the Covenant People.

We covenant ourselves to God in the faithfulness of our actions. This is one of the things that sets the pacifist apart, despite all the meetings where we talk about what will be the effective action to perform. "Should we have this demonstration?" "Should we do this or should we do that?" I sat through those meetings all through the Civil Rights movement and through the anti-Vietnam war movement. Nobody ever knew what would be effective.

But the call to the person of faith is not a call to success; it is a call to faithfulness. We stand for life and give witness to the God of life. Not because we necessarily think it will turn the world around, but because it is what we are called to do and what we MUST do.

You may remember Jeremiah, who predicted the doom of the nation of Judah, that they would be conquered and destroyed. He went out and bought a piece of farmland. That was his affirmation of life and of a future in the face of death and destruction. That was an act of faith. And that is what our witness is to be: an act of faith.

I must say, I am not an optimist. An optimist is someone who says, "Don't worry, everything will be all right." I am worried, and I'm not sure everything's going to be all right. I'm not an optimist, but I HAVE GREAT HOPE. Hope is again, I believe, a matter of faith, a necessity of faith.

Judah ha-Levi, a 12th century Spanish-Jewish philosopher and poet describing the Jewish people said, "We are prisoners of hope." We ARE prisoners of hope. That is different from either the half-baked optimists or the people who hide in a world of illusion and do not confront reality. Who would really say the Pentagon is benign, and the American and Russian empires are benign, and that they are really going to take care of us? That's a world of illusion. But the first and last hope understands what the tremendous obstacles are before us, and DESPITE that, continues to hope. It is Job saying, "Though he slay me, yet will I trust him." That is a religious position.

The fundamentalists, who have a voice through the Moral Majority (which is neither), make it difficult for anybody to read the Bible anymore, because their literalism kills the poetry. The poet says, "The road winds like a ribbon through the hills." The literalist asks, "Where's the ribbon?" They get into a debate about whether it is a silk ribbon or a cotton ribbon, and there is no poetry left.

The Bible is not a consistent doctrine. The Bible is a human document. I believe as Martin Buber teaches, that it is the record of the human encounter with the Divine, and is what flows from that encounter with God.

It is a record of Divine encounter, and it is culturally determined. People live in time and place; they speak a specific language; they have a specific way of relating to the world. I would have to agree with Shakespeare: The devil can cite scripture for the devil's own purposes. I was raised in the South where I listened to the preachers saying that segregation was the will of God. Something deep in me as a small child knew better. But they could cite scripture to prove it. I could not cite scripture, but deep inside of me, through my relation with God, I knew it was not true.

Consequently, when you look at scripture, you find everything in it. You read the record of the Hebrew people, this little feisty people that gets freedom from slavery. Incidentally, Roman Catholic liberation theology grows out of that act – the exodus of the slave people becoming free. For Jews, liberation theology is not news. It is the bedrock of Judaism that God created human beings to be free. God is the God of liberation, who desires human liberation and stands with people struggling for liberation.

You have one strain in the Bible, this feisty little people fighting its way through history; then there's another strain. It starts in the beginning with Father Abraham, who's called *ha'yehudi ha'rishon* – the first Jew. Father Abraham makes his migration from Ur of Chaldea in the Tigris-Euphrates Valley, around the fertile crescent, down into Judah. Father Abraham is a desert sheik, a Bedouin sheik. Nomads like that wander today. When you go to Israel that is what you see – the little tribes migrating, the Bedouins with scraggly goats. That was

7

what it was then too. They were goat herders in their patched up goat skin tents.

Abraham was a very prosperous sheik. He and his nephew, Lot, had large flocks. You remember the story in the Bible? The shepherds of Lot and the shepherds of Abraham are at each other. Abraham says to Lot and his shepherds, "You choose where to go. If you choose the right, then we will go to the left. If you choose the left, then we will go to the right." Abraham in this ancient story is saying: the best land and water are not worth fighting over.

From Abraham on, another strain in the Bible exists parallel with that feisty little people fighting their way to the land of Canaan. This is a strain that we as pacifists identify with and in which we root ourselves. Moses stood on the top of Sinai and had an encounter with God, his mystical experience on top of the mount. I believe the experience is wordless. Whether it is a Christian mystic, or a Jewish mystic, or a Hindu mystic, or a Buddhist mystic, the path to that experience is always culturally conditioned. It is out of time. It is out of space. And it is wordless.

But words flow from experience, the words that flow from Moses' experience culminate in: "Thou Shalt Not Kill." David completes the conquest of the holy land, and the Book of Chronicles tells us that Solomon built the Temple of God. David was not permitted to build the Temple because David was a man who had bloody hands from battle. The Bible is telling us that violence, even the violence of organized armies, comes under the judgment of God.

As we wrestle again with the question of the draft, young people have to confront the draft and decide whether or not to register. If they do, what is going to happen. We confront this with fear and trembling because there has never been a registration without a draft. There has never been a draft without a war. We want to make this time different from all other times. We want to make this the first registration without a draft and the first draft without a war.

There's a draft law in the 20th Chapter of Deuteronomy, the biblical draft law that goes back 3000 years or more. It says that someone who has built a house and not lived in it is exempt from the draft. Someone who has planted a vineyard and not eaten the fruit thereof is exempt from the draft. A man who has betrothed a wife and not consummated the marriage is exempt from the draft. You know what that is saying: that every person is entitled to human fulfillment, that you are entitled to human fulfillment.

When I look at the handful of young people here tonight, I think of the fact that I have been privileged to watch my children grow up. I have had the opportunity to actualize all the parts of myself. I think you are entitled to that. That is why I think all of us have to put stopping the nuclear holocaust at the top of our priority list. Every human being is entitled, if they wish, to marry and, if they wish, to have a child, to watch that child grow up, to get someone else started on a pilgrimage. That's your human entitlement. It says so in the 20th Chapter of Deuteronomy.

If one were to carry through the logic of the 20th Chapter of Deuteronomy, one would say that the minimum draft age would have to be 40. Most of the lawmakers are past 40, and the people who make the laws and have the power should be the ones who decide what they are going to do. It was A. J. Muste who said that to confess someone else's sins is not a religious act. To decide the sacrifice that someone else is going to make is not a religious act either.

The next thing it says in the Deuteronomic draft law is: "AND HE WHO IS AFRAID IS SENT HOME."

The draft law of Deuteronomy turns everything over and looks at it again: What does it mean to be exempt from the army? One of the rabbinic theories in the midrash is that the fear of sinning by killing is a reason for exemption from the draft. You're afraid that you might commit a moral offense in the army. It is simply the doctrine of conscientious objection which was recognized that early. . . .

After the writing of the Bible, Judaism continues and Jews continue to encounter God in their daily experience. From that experience flow more writings; our scriptures are still being written. Martin Buber was writing our scriptures. Abraham Joshua Heschel was writing our scriptures. The process has never ended. We have a new flow of writing of scripture from the first century B.C. The Talmud is then redacted in final edition around 700, and the group of works called the Midrash, which is a homiletical interpretation of the scriptures, continued. These people go back and look at the biblical scriptures and say, "What does it mean?" It's called the Rabbinic period in Jewish history, when the rabbinate develops and the rabbis are the authoritative interpreters of Judaism. The rabbis of that long period are almost all pacifists in their outlook and teachings.

When the children of Israel crossed the Red Sea, they sang a song of triumph, which you'll find in the 15th Chapter of the Book of Exodus. In days when writing was not current, poetry was functional. Poetry was memorable speech. How many paragraphs of prose do you remember? How many poems do you remember? Your poems may be words to a song, because speech reinforced by music is the easiest thing to remember. So the oldest portions of the Bible are poetry. The chapter in Exodus is graphic. It is exciting. It tells you about the Egyptians pursuing the Israelites, about the Egyptians drowning in the Red Sea and sinking like lead, and the waters covering over them. It is graphic. Then it sings praises to God. It says, *"Adonai, Adonai, Ismael H'bavu* – The Lord, the Lord is a man of war." It's not too nice for pacifists, is it?

The ancient rabbis of the *Midrash* had to deal with this. It's not too nice for them either. Here's the story the ancient rabbis tell: "When the children of Israel sang their song of triumph after crossing the Red Sea, the angels in Heaven joined them in singing. God asked the angels, 'Why are you singing?' They said, 'We are singing because your children, the children of Israel have been saved today.' God rebukes them by saying, 'Do you not know that the Egyptians who drowned today are also my children?' "

That is the religious command. Let's face it – I don't care what conflict you read about – there's one side that gets more sympathy than the other one. We do feel a bit of glee if our side is winning. But once we have had that human experience, then somehow or other we have to remember that "the Egyptians who are drowning this day are also my children."

I will tell you a secret about Jews: Jews like to believe

that "Love Your Enemy" is Christian, because it gets us off the hook. But I must tell you that Jesus, who was a Jewish teacher was nowhere near as original as you all think he was. Christians quote Jesus: "Thou shalt love the Lord thy God, and love thy neighbor as thyself." But turn back into the Hebrew scriptures, and you will find that Jesus was teaching Judaism. It's all there; half of it comes from the Fifth Chapter of Deuteronomy, the other half from the 19th Chapter of Leviticus. He was teaching Judaism.

When he was teaching "Love thy neighbor," he was teaching from the Book of Proverbs where it says, "If your enemy hungers, feed him; if he thirsts, give him to drink." The biblical concept of enemy is another human being for whom you are also responsible. You do not get off the hook at all by calling someone your enemy and hating that person, because if the enemy hungers you still have to feed the enemy, and if the enemy thirsts, you still have to give drink.

The biblical name for God, yhvh, is the continuous present, also called the imperfect of the Hebrew word "to be." God is the ever-unfolding of being or becoming, in that name. A group of Protestant theologians today who call themselves process theologians assert that God is the process of the universe. God is the process of being.

If that's okay for God, it's okay for us, too. We do not have to flagellate ourselves because we have not arrived at the perfect state of loving other people. But if we regard ourselves as "process" and know where we're going and work on it, it's okay not to be there yet. Life is journey, not destination.

Pacifists can acknowledge that we are angry sometimes. We have all these other problems that other people have, but we are in process. We know where we are traveling. We are trying to get there, and we are going to struggle to get there. We know the struggle will be a lifelong struggle. We are going to try to make our ideals and our actions find some harmony in the whole process.

Judaism is not a confession of faith, it is a program of action. If you ask someone, "Are you Christian?" they may answer you, "Yes." Or they may say, "I don't know what I believe." That would be a weird answer to the question "Are you Jewish?" because Judaism is not a confession of faith. It's not an issue of I believe this or I don't believe that. It is a program of action. I might answer, "Yes I'm Jewish but I don't do anything about it. I don't observe anything."

The action, the observance, has a word. It's called *mitzvah*. Mitzvah is both the divine commandment as we hear it and our response to that commandment and what we do. It is our calling to string pearls of mitzvot (the plural of mitzvah) for the glory of God—to make a string of our deeds, our actions. Judaism doesn't worry so much about motivation.

The Hebrew verb is an intense form of action. There is no verb "to be" in the present tense in Hebrew, because nothing has happened yet. You've got to do something. You'd say, "this book" but you can't say "this is a book" in Hebrew. There's no verb "is." The Hebrew Bible never asks, "What is God?" The question in the Hebrew Bible is, "What does the Lord require of me? What must I do?" And the task in Hebrew is called *tikun ha'olam*, the repair of the world, or completion of the world. You know, God created human beings, but God never created a perfect human society. That is our task. George Eliot wrote a beautiful poem with a line: "God filled the hills with marble, but God never built a cathedral." There is a human calling: to be partners with God. Martin Buber says the peacemaker is God's partner. That is an ancient Jewish concern. I believe God works on earth through human beings.

The Jewish statement is this: Judaism is against quietism, against the persons who mind their own business, don't bother anybody, about whom neighbors would say, "They take such good care of their family." But they haven't taken care of their family at all. Not until they take care of my family, too. I have to struggle for pure air to breathe, clean water to drink, and a world where my child can have a chance of growing up with some kind of confidence. So what we have to do for our family is going to move us right out of the house.

The Talmud, which was written around 1500 years ago, teaches that whoever is able to protest against the transgressions of their families, whoever is able to protest against the transgressions of their communities, whoever is able to protest against the transgressions of the entire world, and does not do so, is punished for the transgressions of family, and of community and of the entire world. You cannot sit quietly with your mouth closed and escape responsibility. Action is demanded. You are here not only because you are confessors of a beautiful and important way of life, but because you are people who come together in community to work with other people. And God only knows, we need each other.

The work we have to do and the world we have to confront is so discouraging. I pick up the paper everyday. Some times the most depressing part of my day is after reading the paper. I pick up today's paper: they are getting ready to dismantle the Endangered Species Act. All those four-legged animals, the wiggly little things, the flying things, the creeping and crawling things were protected by the laws they're trying to dismantle now. They have not yet enacted a law to protect the human being, who is an endangered species. That is what we are struggling for, isn't it?

Everyday you pick up the paper, and you see the things for which we have been struggling. They are taking them away from us. Our struggle is not over. So we become discouraged. Every time we escalate our action, they escalate theirs. A book, *Running for Depression,* says if your feet are moving it is hard to be depressed. I recommend action for everyone—get together, write letters, take to the streets, resist taxes. We have to escalate our resistance at every turn. It will keep us from being depressed, if nothing more.

The person of faith goes forward, not because there is a guarantee of success, but because we must be witnesses to God's truth. Our calling is to speak truth to power with the voice of love. I don't know if we will be successful or not. I do know that every child I see places a demand that I work for a world for that child to survive in. For life to go on, we must affirm life. If I knew the world was going to be destroyed tomorrow, I would plant a tree today.

Used by permission. Reprinted from the Resource Center for Non-violence Newsletter, Fall 1982, P.O. Box 2324, Santa Cruz, California 95063. Edited for this publication.

THE FUTURE AWAITS

(Can be sung to the tune: "You Light Up My Life")

Cries of the earth come crashing upon me,
The wanting, the striving, the search for the way.
So many dreams were locked deep inside me.
At last we unite in one common quest.

Over the earth people awaken
Claiming the cause — a new world for all.
So many dreams are waiting to happen,
We're linked as one with one destiny.

Facing the future with mixed fear and gladness,
Forging the courage to stand to the end.
So many dreams! A global resurgence
With passion for all we summon the new.

Chorus:
    Now, now is the time,
    Now is our chance
    To care for all
    The future awaits for us
    To build with hope.

Coda:
    Now is our time, the future awaits
    And we'll build a new day.

Song used by permission of the Institute of Cultural Affairs, 4750 North Sheridan Road, Chicago, Illinois, 60640.

BUDDHISM AND THE QUEST FOR WORLD PEACE

by Kenjun Honda

Born in 1907, Kenjun Honda is a priest of the Otani branch of the Shinshu sect of Buddhism. He is chief director of the Japan Buddhist Federation.

His brief statement is included here for two purposes. First, it is a call to Buddhists to be faithful to the basic tenets of their faith and reminds them of the model of loving compassion of the Buddha. We who call ourselves Christians can apply that admonition to our own religious heritage and the reminder that we have the model of Christ to follow. In addition, the statement reminds us that Christians and Jews are not the only religious in the world and that certainly the concern for peace and peace-making is not limited to those who experience the mystery of God the same as we do.

Enlightenment, or *satori,* is the foundation of Buddhist doctrine as well as the pinnacle that Buddhists strive to attain. Japanese Buddhism embraces the tenets of Mahayana Buddhism. It has two particularly important concepts: *jirigyo* and *ritagyo*. This is seeking enlightenment for oneself and for others, respectively. Though seemingly different, they constitute an inseparable entity that is the core of Buddhist philosophy.

A frequently related Buddhist parable tells of a mother whose child had just died. Clutching her child's body, the grief-stricken woman prostrated herself before the Buddha. She begged for relief from her sorrow. I am not sure what words of consolation the Buddha offered her, I am certain that he comforted the bereaved mother in the best way possible, making her grief his own and weeping along with her. In their efforts to attain peace, Buddhists should recall and mirror this loving compassion of the Buddha.

Many Japanese religious leaders, both Buddhists and adherents of other faiths, have admirably endured hardships in the name of achieving peace. However, when religious leaders' efforts for peace rest on an ideological base, they can be less than productive. Buddhists must take care lest the premises of their peace efforts veer from the fundamental teachings of Buddhism, particularly compassion.

Until recently, the rhetoric of discussion on peace invariably included two opposites: war and peace. Today, though, peace is discussed in terms of the survival of humanity versus its destruction. It is tragic that conditions in our world have deteriorated so severely.

The very critical nature of our times demands that we seek a new starting point for our peace movement. This starting point must be unfettered by the values that have affected our efforts thus far. I believe that we should look to religion for this starting point.

One cannot deny that throughout the long history of the human race religion has often sparked conflicts, and does so even today. However, world conditions today demand that people of religion take the initiative in attaining peace. I hope that my fellow Buddhists can draw on basic Buddhist doctrine and renew their pursuit of peace.

Used by permission. Reprinted from "Echoes of Peace," February 1983, The Niwano Peace Foundation, Akasaka Grand House 202, 8-6-17 Akasaka, Minato-ku, Tokyo 107 Japan. Edited for this publication.

His Holiness, Patriarch Pimen and a delegation from The Russian Orthodox Church.

In July 1983, the National Broadcasting Company presented two television programs entitled "The Church of the Russians." Bruce Rigdon, professor of Church History at McCormick Theological Seminary in Chicago, was the narrator for the programs. Peace and the church's relationship to peace were among the many areas of life presented in the program.

In addition to comments on peace by Rigdon, statements are included by Archbishop Makarii of Kiev, Metropolitan Filaret who is chairman of the External Church Relations Department, Patriarch Pimen who is the head of the Russian Orthodox Church, and three women, who did not identify themselves in the interview.

In this portion, peace is described as a universal desire. Peacemaking is a part of the witness of the faithful in the church of Russia. This hope for peace is based on their understanding of the Christian gospel. It also grows out of the experience of people now living of World War II and the millions of their people who died then.

It raises a question about what is appropriate action for Christians. Is it only or primarily being present with people as they suffer through the horror of war? Or, is it to work toward preventing such war?

VOICES FROM RUSSIA

Interview by Bruce Rigdon

Makarii—During the German occupation of Kiev, one of the Kiev monasteries hid in its cells up to 200 Jews of Kiev and wounded Soviet soldiers as well. This was a very dangerous act because Germans would kill not only the Jews found in the monasteries but also the nuns. And so under threat of their own lives, this monastery was giving great service to the people of Kiev...

Rigdon—In this vast and complicated story in a vast and complicated land, there was much to learn about the meaning and function of the major Christian faith. We allowed that church to speak for itself, although we were aware that the issues surrounding the church are complex and could not always be voiced.

Metropolitan Juvenaly of Kolmuna told us about the ongoing contacts with other denominations in the Soviet Union and in other countries.

Metropolitan Alexei, Chancellor of the Patriarchate, told us of the structure of the church, how it chooses governing bodies, about its finances and its theological schools.

But they, and every one of the prelates we interviewed, insisted on confronting the issue of peace.

Metropolitan Filaret, the chairman of the External Church Relations Department, met the question head-on.

Through all history, he said, the Russian Church has inspired the people to defend their homeland—in the days of the Tartars, in the Napoleonic invasion, in the first World War and in the War against Fascism.

Metropolitan Filaret, some people say that peace activities are political. How would you respond to that?

Filaret—The peace activities as well as the ecumenical ones are the matters which are inherent for the church. And we Christians do not need any apology for this kind of activity. We are called to it by our Christian duty and the commandments of the gospel.

I would tell you frankly that at the moment the peacemaking cause of our church just coincides with the foreign policy of our country. And we're glad. But all our peace activity is based on our Christian views. And we do believe that the Christian ideas are common for all humanity.

Rigdon—Patriarch Pimen, the head of the Russian Orthodox Church, agreed to be interviewed in the Patriarch's Palace at Zagorsk. He wanted only to deliver a statement—about peace, his work for peace, the need for friendship and peace between the peoples of his country and the United States. At the end when asked if he had anything else to say, he said, "No." Then he quickly changed his mind and added a postscript:

Pimen—But I will add that I wish for peace. Much, much and much peace! Peace all over!

Rigdon—In a number of places, Russians would approach us and, upon learning who we were, begged to speak to America.

First Woman—My own brother perished during the war.

Second Woman—I would like to tell to the American people that our people not only want peace, they are thirsting for it.

Third Woman—I don't want to see anything like the war again. Certainly we don't want our children to see it.

Rigdon—It was in Leningrad that we were made to understand the depth of this feeling—the all pervasive fear of war among the Soviet people.

Leningrad is itself a war memorial. For 900 days the Nazis laid siege to the city, which refused to surrender despite bombardment and widespread starvation. Every third building was destroyed or badly damaged.

St. Isaac's Museum, formerly a cathedral, still bears the scars of war.

The Winter Palace of the Czars had to undergo extensive restoration.

The Neva River begins at Lake Ladoga, where many men and women drowned trying to drive food trucks across the ice of the lake to the starving city, even when the ice was thawing and could no longer support the weight of their trucks.

At the rear of Nicholsky Cathedral is a churchyard for the military heroes of Leningrad. Some of their graves are marked with parts of their tanks or airplanes.

Every family in Leningrad lost someone—a son, a parent, a sister.

The Eternal Flame memorial was built around the mass graves. There were far too many to identify or bury separately.

We've discovered that it is impossible to talk for very long with the leaders of the Russian Orthodox Church or with faithful members of the church without recognizing that one of their fundamental and passionate concerns is that of peacemaking. Many times also in the few weeks we heard bishops and metropolitans as well as crowds of the faithful who surrounded us wherever we went quote to us that familiar phrase from the Gospels: "Blessed are the peacemakers, for they shall be called the children of God."

It's not simply because it is part of the New Testament that these people appear to care so deeply about peace. Nor is it simply the result of Soviet propaganda, as perhaps so many of us would be inclined to think. More than 22 million Soviet citizens died during the Second World War. Nearly a million of them died in Leningrad. And just as Jews remember the Holocaust as something that is fundamental to their identity in the modern world, so the suffering of the Soviet people is a living reality for them and certainly not forgotten by the church which was so much part of that suffering.

MARCH ONWARD NOW

(Can be sung to the tune: "Bella Ciao")

Oh, we awaken the human vision.
March onward now to the cry of all history.
Resurgent spirit is now emerging,
Giving form to the new community.

We are engagers of human caring.
March onward now in the task to set people free.
Local passion bursts forth in power,
Giving form to the new community.

We are proclaimers of life's abundance.
March onward now placing hope in the mystery.
The human drama reveals the wonder,
Giving form to new possibility.

The world before us, the future open,
March onward now to create the new century.
Human structures that forge a life style,
To give form and release new destiny.

Song used by permission of the Institute of Cultural Affairs, 4750 North Sheridan Road, Chicago, Illinois, 60640.

THE PEACE OF CHRIST IS A DIFFERENT PEACE

by Dorothee Soelle

Dorothee Soelle is a theologian and peace movement activist. She teaches one semester each year at Union Theological Seminary in New York City and the other semester at the University of Hamburg.

In the fall of 1982, she delivered an address at a peace symposium at the College of Wooster in Ohio. This article is drawn from that address. In it, Soelle contrasts Pax Romana with Pax Christi of the Luke Christmas story and then applies that perception of the world to our present situation. Her vision is that unilateral disarmament is consistent with the peace of God of which the Bible speaks.

Dorothee Soelle grew up in Germany in the thirties. She was 15 years old when World War II ended. The culture in which she was nurtured was a refined one with literature, philosophy and music playing an important part in it. Goethe and Rilke, Kant and Schubert were in that world. Her parents were liberals and outspokenly anti-nazi.

She developed and is part of a work group in Cologne, West Germany, whose members seek to bring together faith and practice.

Two entirely different concepts of peace show up in the story of the birth of Jesus as it is told in Luke's Gospel. In the very first part of this Christmas Gospel we hear about Caesar Augustus' decree that all the world should be enrolled for purposes of taxation.

Joseph and Mary have to travel from Nazareth to Bethlehem because of this enrollment. It is a legal measure of the Roman emperor in order to exploit and keep under control the subjected inhabitants of the Roman provinces. The Roman administration had to get hold of the people in these provinces, to register and enlist them.

This measure was a part of a system which was called the peace of Rome, or *Pax Romana.* It consisted of a center, which was Rome, and a periphery, made up of the conquered provinces. In the center of this world order there were material abundance, greed for new goods and pleasures, immorality, psychic emptiness and lack of human feeling. On the edges of this order, in the dominated provinces, there were unbelievable misery and lack of food, water, shelter, work and education. An apathetic hopelessness existed among masses of impoverished people. The hired workers in the vineyard in Jesus' parable (Matt. 20:1-16) who wait all day long to be hired mirror the economic situation. Many other texts of the new Testament talk about the landless and possessionless masses, about their hunger and their diseases. The historical situation of all these stories is the *Pax Romana,* the Roman peace built upon domination over the impoverished. It was a well-perfected system constituted so that the rich could become richer and the poor become poorer. It was called Peace, "pax," by those who loved it and profited from it.

But the story in Luke 2 talks also about a different peace. This peace is announced to poor persons. Peace on earth does not simply mean peace in heaven after this life. It does not simply mean peace with God within your individual soul. It means that the Peace of Christ begins here with poor individuals who have buried their hopes a long time ago. This other peace leads the shepherds from hopelessness and fear into a "great joy which will come to all people." (Luke 2.10) The *Pax Christi* is the good news for all who suffer under the *Pax Romana.* It is news that later will reach the center.

This different peace is not built upon oppression and military domination. It leads the people who seek it into persecution. The messengers of Christ's peace are silenced or not listened to. They are persecuted, and if necessary, eliminated by the state's police, as Paul was. There are many ways to silence people and to make them believe in the system of *Pax Romana.* The background of the Christmas story is the financial politics of Caesar Augustus. He and Pontius Pilate stand at the beginning and at the end of Jesus' story. Specialists in taxation, enrollment and torture, they represent Roman power. It was an organized system of violence and militarism necessary to exploit the people of the provinces and maintain luxury for a few in Rome.

These are two very different concepts of peace. The military peace of Rome starts with intimidation through bureaucracy. The peace of love is among people with whom God is pleased, namely and especially poor people.

One cannot understand the New Testament without keeping in mind the difference between Pax Romana and Pax Christi. We cannot have it both ways. Christians cannot have the peace of Christ in our hearts and for our inner selves while the Pax Romana guarantees our lifestyle and the continuation of the world order in which we live.

When I learned history, the textbooks spoke about the glory and beautiful culture of the Pax Romana. No one told us about the persons who were blind, lame, crippled and sick who you find on almost every page of the New Testament. The whole education I got echoed the Roman propagandists. They called the subjugation of other people "peace," the exploitation "order" and those who were opposed to this system "terrorists."

But in reality, terror was a major means to keep this sort of peace. Any peace built on militarism works through terror. The permanent preparation for war, the preparedness to kill, is called in strategic terms "deterrence." But in the word "deterrence" there is embedded the word terror. The means to keep the world under the domination of Rome were taxation, economic dictatorship, price control and counter-insurgency, including torture, interrogation and militarism. The Pax Romana was a terrorist system. It meant living at a sub-subsistence level in a day-to-day war for survival for the majority of the then known world.

If we look around our own world, we can easily see that

there is a war going on right now. The war between the rich and the poor. According to the most moderate estimation there are 15,000 people each day "falling" in this war. They die from hunger and other curable diseases. The bombs which we produce in preparing ourselves for war are falling now on the poor.

In those days the Roman propagandist, historians say, called the system "peace." They named Caesar the "peacemaker" as seen on Roman coins. Jesus took this word away from those who misused it for their peace and gave it to those who work and live for a different kind of peace. "Blessed are the peacemakers," he said to women, fisherfolk and other ordinary people. It was not the Pax Romana he had in mind. For him, peacemaking did not mean to terrorize people through militarism.

The peace of Christ, the Pax Christi, is built on justice. There is no other way to truly have peace. We have to choose which kind of peace we seek and work for.

THE FUTURE SHAPES THE PRESENT

Today's Pax Romana is based on the ideology of deterrence. *"Si vis pacem, para bellum,"* as the late Roman war historian Flavius Vegetius Renatus put it. Translated, he said, "If you want peace, prepare for war."

. . . . It is not that simple in the time in which we live. The future that we design and deliberately plan changes our present. The militarization of a whole society destroys the memory of their history of liberation. Germans should remember the liberation from fascism and militarism they experienced in 1945. But, with memory, hope dies, too.

. . . . Therefore, some religious leaders in the first world recognize that in a nuclear age the preparation for war, not just its making, is a crime. The possession of nuclear arms, not only their usage, is a sin. . . .

Armaments kill even without war. This is obvious in three areas. Primarily armaments kill the poor people in the third world who cannot be fed with bombs. Secondly, there are disenfranchised people in the rich countries, such as jobless persons, migrant workers and persons with handicapping conditions. The bombs are falling precisely on them. Military rearmament dictates social disarmament. This is happening now in the United States. Underprivileged persons are being robbed of their rights and pushed back into their pre-Roosevelt state of disenfranchisement.

Thirdly, the bombs are falling on the minds and hearts of ordinary people in the first world. They believe in the balance of deterrence and work and pay for the bomb. Among them are the 50 percent of the world's scientists and engineers who do their research for military-related industries, namely for Death. The Bomb is not only something out there, in the Sierra Nevadas or the Pentagon, it is already in our own lives.

The arms buildup destroys every aspect of our lives. What is the sense of an institution like a school if army officers have free access to it? How can someone within the health care system take part in disaster training in triage? How can they divide victims into "don't bother," "not yet" and "to be treated?" How can a government official such as Defense Minister Apel of the Federal Republic of Germany, whose job is to calculate megatons

of dead people, deliver a speech in memory of the victims of World War II on Memorial Day?

Every form of preparation for the use of nuclear violence destroys those who "prepare" themselves. An old pacifist song says, "I ain't gonna study war no more." It's right. "To study war" is more than preparation for later or never. It is practice in shooting, becoming accustomed to the possibility of catastrophe. "Thinking the unthinkable" is not just a simulation game for staff officers. To keep the loyalty of the masses, it must become a principle of education.

Nuclear armament has a total quality, similar to Hitler's "total war."

. . . . A culture dominated by militarism, in its science, its technology and its economy, has increasingly totalitarian tendencies. For a political ideology of "national security," people in Latin America may be tortured. In West Germany they may be barred from their professions, criminalized and slandered. A postal employee who belongs to the Communist Party represents a "security risk." But it is clear that the millions of people who are involved in the peace movement also represent a "security risk." Continuation of the present policy demands sharpened internal repression and decreased democracy.

The conservatives aren't really wrong when they claim that longing is a major characteristic of the peace movement. Granted, they hardly know what longing really is, what lies in its power. To put it down, they qualify it as "only" or "just" longing. In so doing, they fail to recognize the religious dimension of the peace movement in action. They don't understand people are seeking God when they become "resistance fighters against death," as the 19th century religious socialist Christoph Blumhardt called the Christians. One cannot seek God while preparing for mass murder as a precaution. We cannot truly love each other under the domination of militarism.

GOD'S UNILATERALISM

God wills life in abundance, for all people. "I am come that they might have life, and that they might have it more abundantly." (John 10:10) Where God works through people and people live as "lovers of life" as God does, they participate in God's work of creating justice and peace. Peacemaking in this sense has a quality of unilateral action, of risk which is embedded in any creative activity.

What happens to peace under the "balance of deterrence" is that it becomes "business as usual." It is based on bilateral agreement, arms control treaties, summit conferences, which all follow the same pattern. Each politician is careful to hold on to as many deadly toys as possible while swindling the other side out of as many as possible. But is this philosophy of peace enough? All this so-called "balance" has accomplished so far is a permanent state of escalation. Arms controls have been counterproductive because outlawing some weapons permitted the invention of others.

Peace based in terror is obviously not peace. But the middle-class assumption that peace can be brought about through "treaties" contains a kind of naive rationalism. As though people could hold talks without talking with each other, or make deals without dealing with each

Photo: UPI

other, or negotiate before taking action. Only a superficial love of peace praises peace on both sides. Real peace education goes beyond business deals. The arms buildup kills. Bilateralism is nothing more than business. Isn't it conceivable that some things might not be for sale?

A conflict between individuals can perhaps be eased and made more bearable though agreements, deals, mutual consideration. But only if one of the partners moves out of the stalemate can some things change and the conflict be solved. That will happen only if one of them doesn't insist that the situation remain as it is. One side must muster the strength for unilateral action. One of the partners in the dispute must love peace deeply enough to really put away weapons, to really disarm. Preventing violence through the threat of violence doesn't change the existing strife. A first step on the part of someone acting independently of others is constructive and can lead somewhere.

Preparation for nuclear war is a crime according to international law and to the laws of the Federal Republic of Germany. The fact or the assumption that others are committing the same crime makes it no less criminal than pretending war is "defense." It's a question of overcoming bilateral thinking. Only those who unilaterally act for peace really know what it's about. The more articulate the peace movement becomes, the more clearly we see the idea of unilateral refusal of violence.

The most important mental progress I have made over the last few years...is the step from bilateralism to unilateralism. I learned that my hope for bilateral arms limitation was superficial, not serious.

I find an existential lack of seriousness in bilateral thinking. It sounds like the scream of worried mothers: "Quit fighting, Children!" Thus we lie ourselves into the position of obs␣rvers. It's the fault of the fighting children. But in reality we are involved. We pay for the madness. We put up with it. We elect the directors of the madhouse who are responsible for us. We, the innocent, taxpaying citizens, are part of the murderous system. With the system's help, we let poor persons die. If we really want peace then we have to start where we are, on this side. It is neither better nor worse than the other, but whose only truth is that it is our side.

We have to begin unilaterally to be able to move on bilaterally. Anything new begins unilaterally. Nuclear pacifism as the moral-political minimum won't be dealt, calculated and weighed out. There are some things which are existential in that you can't do them with reference to other people.

For example, in religion it doesn't matter what you know about other folks and their relationship to God. What you do is what matters. Anything existential is necessarily one-sided. Peace is an existential category. Many people, above all young people, mistrust politicians. One reason is that they don't believe these persons are capable of peace, because they turn peace into a business. They act like business persons who deal in fear.

In contrast to this, the peace movement has a spirituality which cannot accept this insult to yesterday's dead, this crime against today's poor. The political issue of peace, in connection with issues of imperialism or solidarity with the third world, becomes something which can't be delegated to peace technocrats. It is this depth of personal involvement and vulnerability among those in the peace movement that sends people into the streets and into countless groups, initiatives and individual actions. It is as though people were defensing themselves against being locked into an Orwellian bunker.

The thesis "armaments kill, even without war" has, as I understand it, a theological dimension. Perhaps one cannot understand it without believing at least a little bit in God. Unilateral disarmament is a genuinely religious act of trust in God. The inner strength of the peace movement is that people have chosen God over the bomb. They have chosen Christ's peace over the *Pax Americana-Sovietica* and life over death.

Faith is the peace of *shalom*, which is grounded in justice and implies happiness. Faith is hope for the future of the human family and unconditional love of all that lives. These are experiences and visions that go beyond the given and visible. Therefore the tradition calls faith, hope and love "supernatural virtues." They presuppose the emphatic notion of life with which the Bible operates.

"Life" means more than mere survival against the balance of terror. No one can sell people on acquiescence to the capacity for nuclear blackmail by calling it "insuring peace." "The peace of God which passes all understanding preserve our hearts and minds in Christ Jesus." (Phil. 4:17) This peace which surpasses our calculation is not an inner state of harmony into which the individual can withdraw. It is a peace which is "in the world, but not of the world," which gains ground here and grows into a political strength in the peace movement, but does not develop out of a capitalist mentality. The arms buildup kills. It is the peace that "this" world produces. We need a different peace, because we still need a different world.

Used by permission. Reprinted from "Christianity and Crisis," December 13, 1982, New York, N.Y. Edited for this publication.

Channels of God's Peace

D.R.F.

Donald R. Frederick

1. We would be chan-nels of God's_ peace: Search-ing the ways of
2. God make us mir-rors of your_ peace, Catch-ing your rays of

love,_____ Pray-ing that strife and war-fare shall cease,
love._____ Trou-bled in heart, we claim your re-lease:

Em-powered from heav'n a-bove._____ We would be pil-grims
The peace from God a-bove._____ Trans-form our swords to

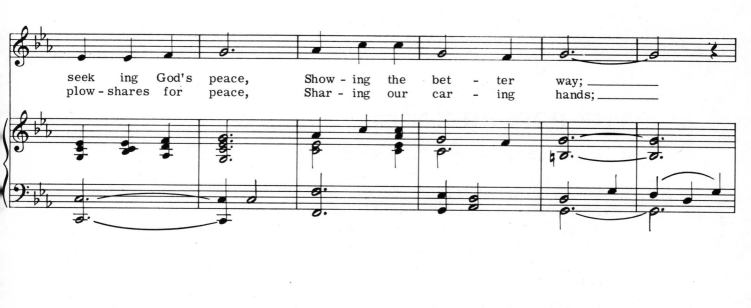

seek ing God's peace, Show - ing the bet - ter way;_____
plow - shares for peace, Shar - ing our car - ing hands;_____

God's Spir - it aids our faith to in - crease, Strength - ens our
Cleanse us from hate, our mal - ice e - rase; Bless, too, our

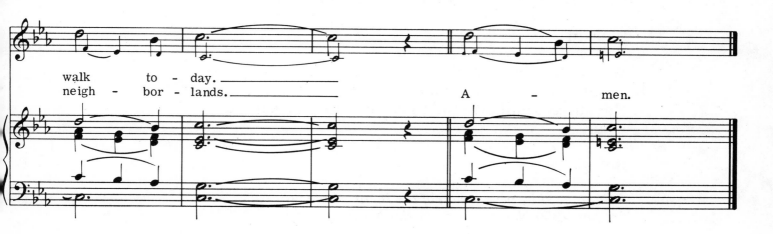

walk to - day._____
neigh - bor - lands._____ A - men.

Channels of God's Peace - 2

THE POSSIBLE NOW

(Can be sung to the tune: "Widdecombe Fair")

The signs of the times are so clearly defined—
  Nationwide, world around and locally.
They demand a response to needs of humankind
  with...

Refrain:
Past sharing—now caring—future bending—life
expending
Work demanding—time to see—
  the possible now that can be,
  The possible now that can be.

The problems that face every one throughout life—
  Nationwide, world around and locally,
Bring cries for relief from the tension and strife
  with...

Refrain

The path stretched before us is no easy road—
  Nationwide, world around and locally,
But corporate spirit will lighten the load with...

Refrain

We know that the task will have no final end—
  Nationwide, world around and locally,
But success will demand that once more we extend
  our...

Refrain

Song used by permission of the Institute of Cultural Affairs, 4750 North Sheridan Road, Chicago, Illinois, 60640.

A VISION OF AN APPROPRIATE SECURITY SYSTEM

by Robert C. Johansen

In the next article Robert C. Johansen talks about his vision of peace—a world without weapons based on an international system. The vision may seem really far away to most people. It would require many of the elements that Soelle has just discussed—a willingness to take courageous action and to trust.

Johanson lists the requirements of this non-weapons based security system. Then he does some deliberate daydreaming about the differences it could make in our world.

This article was part of a paper prepared in 1978 for the Grenville Clark Project on Disarmament, Security and Abolition of the War System. The whole document was also issued as a working paper of the World Order Models Project. In the paper, before stating his vision which we include here, Johansen described our present insecurity, the failure of present policies and the need for system change.

A 1983 edition of the monograph includes a foreword in which the trends and suggestions of the original piece are reinforced by events which have happened in the ensuing five years.

It is difficult to envision a world without war. But, it is no more difficult than imagining world after war. The expectation of war and the presumed necessity of arms exert a strong hold on our consciousness.

Yet if we are to initiate positive social change, it is essential to boldly define the minimum requirements for a security system that functions without war. We must define these requirements regardless of how long it will take to meet them. These essentials are listed below. They may, upon first reading, seem beyond the realm of possibility. Widespread changes in education and attitude can be stimulated by a global social movement. If this happens the limits of the possible could widen sufficiently to achieve a new system with the following characteristics:

1. All nations are protected against the threat or use of violence by any other nation.

2. Such protection can be guaranteed in part because the production and the possession of all military weapons are prohibited. (Law-enforcement equipment necessary for the maintenance of domestic tranquility is, of course, not prohibited.) Extremely hazardous non-weapons materials are also strictly regulated, according to universally applied regulations. These non-weapons include such things as fissionable substances.

3. A world security organization functions with the power to enforce the rules against the possession of weapons or the misuse of fissionable materials. It presides over enforcement activities of a transnational police force. It also administers the arms-reducing process in its final stages. Officials acting on its behalf have the authority to prevent weapons violations anywhere in the world. The organization, operating within a system of checks and balances to insure accountability, is responsible to a global assembly.

4. A global monitoring agency inspects for violations of weapons prohibitions. Information regarding possible violations can be given directly to the agency by any citizen of any country.

5. Countries are required to settle disputes through nonviolent political, social or judicial processes.

6. A standing, individually recruited transnational police or peace force enforces the globally established rules for war prevention.

7. The diversion of resources from the manufacture of military equipment into the production of food. The abolition of poverty enables most families on earth to have adequate nourishment and shelter.

Once the movement for an appropriate security system is well advanced, other changes, which are unrealistic by today's standards, would become genuine possibilities:

Prolonged unemployment could be eliminated by utilizing the potential for global economic cooperation and by diverting investment capital from military production to civilian production that generates more jobs.

Beaches, streams, lakes and the atmosphere could recover from an overload of toxic wastes. A portion of funds previously allocated for military expenditures would be used for environmental protection.

Conflicts among nations with different ideologies would continue to be intensely waged. But as now occurs domestically in some societies, they would be waged only in nonviolent ways.

Local and urban governments could experience rejuvenation because the money and talent formerly attracted to weapons production could be applied to their needs. Among the problems addressed could be the development of alternative sources of energy, urban planning, mass transit, adult education and elimination of unemployment and crime. Also, military influence would decline. Violence in national security policies would be eliminated. Thus, national governments would lose the single largest component of their dominance over state and local government. In the United States there would be less basis for the largess which allows national institutions to exert control over communities and congressional districts across the country. Local governments in many nations might receive more citizen attention, resulting in improved quality.

People could feel less alienated from other nationalities. There would be no need to be ready and willing to destroy generic brothers and sisters in Moscow on fifteen minutes notice. Nor could people need to fear that their wheat or computer components sold abroad will help some "foreigners" gain military advantage over them. Travel could be less encumbered by political and military chauvinism.

There would be pervasive internal consequences for some militarized societies. Military dictators and racist regimes would be deprived of one of their major rationales for existence, security needs. They would no longer need the military hardware they have used to maintain their power. Starting the process to abolish the hardware system would give new life to human rights efforts around the world.

Military dominance in world affairs could not continue without large national arsenals. Therefore, forms of non-military influence would take on new importance. The industrial giants would continue to possess great power. However, the presently weak nations would no longer suffer the disadvantage of being militarily inferior.

The advance of human rights and global self-determination would be aided by the demise of covert political interventions from groups like the CIA and KGB. Such activities would no longer be justified on national security grounds. Overseas collaborators would not be so readily found in a climate where military regimes no longer prospered.

A decline in the role of military power would also contribute to economic justice. To be sure, the economically powerful societies would not be much more eager to share wealth. With military power and with covert intervention diminished, the rich would be less able to force their will on the persons who are poor. Rich elites could no longer rationalize opposition to social reformers on grounds that the latter were a threat to national security. The success of a new ideology in any country could not become a military threat to its neighbors.

Favorable though most of the prospects sound, such a world would be no utopia. There doubtless would be controversies over establishing trade and immigration policies, transferring technology, pricing food and energy resources, and disposing of hazardous wastes. There would be fears that one society might develop powerful non-military means for exerting dominance over other groups. Some disputes will arise that are presently unforeseen. Yet, all of these conflicts will exist even if we continue the arms buildup. Resolving them will be far easier if nations are securely unarmed than if they are armed. The proposed system will establish a better climate for cooperation and make available more resources than a global system heavily burdened by armaments.

A global peace system clearly seems desirable. What strategy could make it possible?

THE FIRST DAY OF HOPE

by Betty Reardon   *June 1990*

Picture a huge arena located in a place not on the North American continent. Betty Reardon gives some clues in the last paragraph of the story of the possible location for the celebration of the inauguration of the World Disarmament Plan.

Note the date of this journal writing—June 1990. That is only a few years away. One reason why this piece is included is because it provides a picture of the future that does have hope. It also appears possible. All the events and individuals mentioned prior to 1982 are real. The events have happened. The people have made their witness. Also based in reality are some of the persons described as participants in the ceremony in the stadium. All the events described as occurring after 1983 are just as possible as a nuclear detonation.

Betty Reardon is program director of the Peacemaking in Education program of United Ministries in Education. She teaches with others of the faculty of Teachers College, Columbia University, a continuing symposium on educating for peacemaking and leads a two-week international institute in that area each summer. Reardon works actively with the World Council for Curriculum and Instruction, a transnational association of educators with members in all regions of the world and was its executive secretary. She also works actively with the International Peace Research Association as well as with the world Policy Institute, formerly the Institute for World Order.

It was cool and clear in the stadium this morning. The sunlight was so bright. I felt as if I could see the past and future as clearly as I saw the present. I could see places other than this huge arena thousands of miles from my New York home. From that home I had viewed the events leading to this formal inauguration of the World Disarmament Plan.

How had all this been possible when less than a decade ago we had been so close to unprecedented destruction? When did it start to happen? What was the turning point? Where did the vision come from that gave me this sense of *deja vu?*

Only once before had I seen or experienced anything like today. I scanned the stadium near where I was sitting with the observers. The faces and garb reflected the varieties of human diversity. That diversity had recently and vigorously been reclaimed. It had almost disappeared into the homogenization of the global military—industrial culture.

The sight reminded me of the huge auditorium of the Medical Center in Mexico where the Womens Tribunal met in June 1975. Then I thought about the great assembly in another part of Mexico City at that same time where the formal U.N. conference convened. Then as today, the delegates filed into their section. Many of them embraced, shaking hands. They greeted each other with the enthusiasm of members of a winning team. Theirs was the energy of those revitalized by ultimate success in a long and arduous struggle.

The official delegates at that 1975 event were somewhat more decorous than we nongovernmental observers were. Some of us were members of a variety of organizations and movements. Others were totally unaffiliated participants in the struggle.

Most of us had contributed to "stalling traffic" in the large tunnel entrances—shouting, waving to each other, hugging, blowing kisses. No small number did dances of joy as they sang their way to their places in the stand. Even the delegates seemed joyous.

Maybe the source for our experience today was there on those hot and rainy days. Our feet were constantly wet from waiting for the bus to take us for our nearly daily trips from the nongovernmental tribune to the official U.N. conference to lobby the delegates. We struggled to assure that some consideration of the legitimate concerns of women would be included in the politics-as-usual discourse of the nation-states. Ah, the startled look of the grey-garbed Chinese delegate as she emerged from the toilet stall to have a disarmament statement thrust at her! We were determined to focus attention on disarmament as the basic requirement for "peace." Without that we saw little hope for the two other themes of that international year that became a U.N. decade — "equality" and "development."

Memory carried me back to the tribunal and the panel on disarmament. A Nobel Laureate received a standing ovation from the women when he told them the task was theirs. He asserted that without their persistent, global, and voluminous demand, the male power structures of the nation-states would never disarm. He declared, "If you have to take to the streets, do it! And keep doing it until we've got an agreement for General and Complete Disarmament!" General and Complete Disarmament (GCD) was his watchword.

He and others who clearly perceived the true dangers to human security constantly articulated this same vision. Complete disarmament, he said, was the only real hope for peace and the fundamental need for survival. He also continuously pointed to the need, as he did in his call to the women, to articulate the demands forcefully and publicly. He called for the legitimate expression of popular sovereignty in public opinion. He pointed to the potential for articulation and execution of the "will of the people" that lay in communications media free of the control of nation-states.

Maybe the media is what really made the difference. Certainly without it there would not have been the great outpouring of revulsion at the thought of nuclear war and the rejection of further development of nuclear weapons. Without the media, that threat would not have been responded to by the policy-makers, especially the leaders of the nuclear states and most especially the superpowers.

Yes, the media's coverage of the shift in doctrine from deterrence to limited nuclear war policy was significant. The politicians did not expect the masses of people to notice or respond to the message of the media. The politicians assumed they could continue to cover it over with arguments about national security and technical competence. All their smoke screens had for so long kept the average person from confronting the fundamental security issues.

Surely that response of the politicians had an impact. They had made the mistaken assumptions of a leadership out of touch with the people, in fact out of touch with reality. The shift startled and frightened even those of us in the peace movement. Even the researchers who had closely followed arms issues and were always aware of the grave danger were surprised. It made the danger more imminent. We could see it, smell it, feel it, almost touch it. The danger was constantly in our heads. It often crowded out all other thoughts. It screamed "Do something! Act on your knowledge! Live your commitment!" And that was part of it, too.

Large numbers of people began to live by their commitment to the reversal of militarization and the abolition of war. Some even willingly died for this goal. The deaths were not as the innocent victims of militarism and repression, but as persons consciously embracing the ultimate risk for the sake of the ultimate value. But again, without the media would so many have known of these martyrs— a few American religious, a Dutch journalist, and the others?

None of them had to be there with their lives on the line in the struggle. Nor in fact did all the others about whom we never learned because neither their lives nor their deaths were considered "newsworthy." Now people demanded to know.

Yes, it might be that public opinion can influence the media as much as the other way around. Even journalists can have commitments and be both acclaimed and reviled for them. I thought briefly of the Jonathan Schell phenomenon and the startling impact of his book on people who had never thought seriously about the problem of nuclear war.[1] After the book came the great stir in the media and conversation which reflected the chastening effect. Then came the denial, "Oh, well, nothing new in it after all." "Very badly written, don't you think?" "Oh, yeah, typical *New Yorker* verbosity." "There simply can't be total devastation. Something, someone will survive to build anew." "Indeed, where there is life there is hope."

Ah, but that possibility could not be fully denied. There could, in fact, be no *reflective* life left, arrogant as that may seem to roaches and rodents. That was it....This time the hope was born out of the realization that there could be no life, out of the determination to prevent the death of the planet.

Yet none of this could have happened without the visions and the plans to make realities out of possibilities. Needed were the strategies and policies to capitalize on the tiny flickering lights of hope during those very days when the trends toward global militarization were so virulent.

Yesterday on the plane, I was in a seat separated from the others in my chapter of Educators for Social Responsibility (ESR).[2] ESR was one of the many observer groups traveling to witness this culminating ceremony, though most of us know it is only the beginning. As we traveled, I remembered my distant past as a student and teacher of history. I jotted down a chronology of the political events that got us to today's affirmation ritual. This goal had so often seemed at best impractical, and, at worst, impossible. The goal was distant even to those of us who kept insisting we could stop the arms race saying it was only a matter of "political will."

I did not bother to record the long history of disarmament efforts from the mid-nineteenth century, so frequently reviewed with students. Nor did I start with the international treaties of the nuclear age. These treaties were all too often cited as proof of the effectiveness of arms control agreements.[3]

Instead, I pulled from the roots of history, read or remembered, some 20th century landmarks on the road toward the abolition of war, toward the popularization and realization of the notion of general and complete disarmament. My chronology...went like this.

1928	Kellogg Briand Pact—renounces war as an instrument of national policy—signed by 50 nations.
1932	World Disarmament Conference meets in Geneva—recognized arms race as a cause of war.
1945	U.N. Charter declares as its purpose putting an "end to the scourge of war." First resolution of the General Assembly prohibits the use of nuclear weapons.
1945	Japan dissolves its military.
1948	Costa Rica abolishes its army; transfers funds to education.
1950-1963	U.N. peacekeeping actions undertaken.
1975	International Womens Year (IWY) catalyzes international women's movement for disarmament.
1978	U.N. First Special Session on Disarmament (SSDI) designates total elimination of national military forces as long-range goal of disarmament.[4]
1979-82	Shift in strategic doctrines discloses seriousness of possibility of nuclear war.
1980	UNESCO convenes World Congress on Disarmament Education. European women present disarmament petition with thousands of signatures to Secretary General at Women's Mid-Decade Conference.
1981-82	Massive demonstrations for nuclear disarmament take place in Europe, Japan, Australia, North America, June 1982. Convening of Second Special Session on Disarmament (SSDII) becomes focal point for coordinated worldwide popular movement for disarmament.
1983	Launching of U.N. World Disarmament campaign to educate and mobilize the general public in favor of disarmament.[5]
1984-86	U.N. Peacekeeping Force established as member states initiate reduction of arms and armed forces having adopted the Defensive Weapons System.[6]
1985	Regional Development—Disarmament Councils established in all world regions

to guide economic conversion of resources and production from the military to civilian sectors and to assure security through the fulfillment of human needs.

1987   Third Special Session on Disarmament outlines a basic treaty for general and complete disarmament.

JUNE 1990   Final ratification of the World Treaty on General and Complete Disarmament. Massive worldwide celebration—with the coming international ceremony to mark its coming into force.

Long before yesterday's review, the events leading here seemed clear to me. Even as they happened I had seen them off as landmarks on my mental map of the journey to disarmament. Still, I could not put my finger on what one event had really made the difference. I kept looking around the stadium. I searched out individual faces of people I knew had been important in the movement. I also spotted representative groups recognized as significant political forces. I focused on the bright yellow robes of a Japanese Buddhist monk standing at one of the entrances to the playing field. He was holding a round single-skin drum of a type that had set the rhythm for another week in June years ago.

More clergy began to cluster around him. They prepared themselves to walk out onto the platform on the middle of the field where the opening religious observation was to take place. In my memory, I heard again the pulse of those drums, blending into the guitars and crisp voices of the young Benedictines singing in the Cathedral of St. John the Divine in New York City. Ten thousand people representing virtually every spirit and religious tradition crammed the entire space of the huge nave. Hearing the mental replay of those sounds reawakened the strong feelings of human solidarity and the spiritual energy released that day in 1982.

The world religions have played a vital role in the struggle. More than any other single force in the movement, they demonstrated the ability to transcend cultural, political and ideological differences. It was religious people who manifested the courage to articulate fundamental moral principles in the face of political pragmatism. Their convergence into the single world force for peace and disarmament had come from small, fragmentary beginnings.

I thought for an instant of a church basement in Brooklyn where another saffron-robed monk from Japan had spoke, simply but with passion. I was in a group of no more than 15 people. It was less than a year before the gathering of the 10,000 in 1982.

We sat then at folding tables across the United States. Beside me was a Colombian Catholic priest. Next to him sat the Lutheran pastor of the church. I had never seen that Lutheran pastor before, but we knew one another. We spoke to each other out of the sense of closeness that comes from a common struggle. I had known the priest with us over the decade since a small seminar in Mexico had brought together a handful of educators from the United States and Latin America. We had explored there the possibilities of cooperative efforts in peace education.

These small meetings, these tentative connections and common endeavors, built a worldwide network of people

of very different backgrounds and life circumstances who shared similar hopes, fears and visions. Although they were not together often, people forged a community of caring. This community gave support and courage to its members. The courage to continue in the face of setback after setback was undoubtedly the essential ingredient in the whole recipe of the disarmament struggle.

That courage was evident when some in the religious establishment saw the need to return to the prophetic role of religion. They began to articulate what many were beginning to feel about the meaning of nuclear weapons and the international system that had produced them at so great a cost to the entire human family.

As nations marched blindly from one stage of military preparedness to the next "advance in weapons technology," military values took precedence over humane norms. In the early 1980s the churches spoke out forcefully against the irrationality and evil of nuclear weapons, the arms race and the militarization process. The churches gave popular voice to the ethical choice only a few scientists and philosophers had recognized in the early years of the "atomic age."[7] The churches had been in the forefront, too, in organizing the massive demonstrations against nuclear weapons and war which took place in cities all over the world in the early 1980s.

The clergy gathered, preparing to file onto the platform on this historic day. I noticed a young women wearing a clerical collar above a dark blue bib. Her companion wore a heavy cross and chain. I took her to be a Catholic sister. Their presence in that gathering represented the significant merger between feminist politics and the peace movement. They also represented millions of women who

25

had worked in their own communities to educate people to the dangers of nuclear war and the possibilities of peace.

I thought of the letter I had received about 10 years ago from a young friend in Oxford, England, the mother of an eight-year-old girl.

This woman had wanted a future for her child. She had surprised even herself by beginning to make public speeches, first in her own village, then in other small communities across England. She and other mothers began to instruct themselves as they stood in the play yard watching their children.

They knew the chances of their children becoming adults diminished with each technological weaponry advance. She formed a national movement similar to that being organized by women all over the world. In her letter she had told me of the four women who met around a kitchen table in Copenhagen about a year before the U.N. Mid-Decade Women's Conference was to meet there in 1980. Those four women began the European Women for Peace movement. A high point of this movement was presenting a peace petition to the Secretary General of the United Nations.

Indeed women nurtured and cultivated the grass-roots peace movement. They stood on U.S. street corners with Freeze petitions.[8] They traveled across Europe in second-class night trains to meet with sisters in other cities. They talked without formal translation or the professional and diplomatic support systems that facilitate international dialogue.

Their support system was their own commitment to the future of their children. Their facilities were their own energies and convictions. They believed the struggle for women's equality and the struggle for world peace were one. This was an insight that for so long many found hard to comprehend. Even those who contributed analysis of the situation as a basis for political strategies were slow to comprehend. Indeed, many still find it hard to understand.

Yes, many of us in this struggle have had our blind spots. Particular individual and political divisions had often threatened to shatter the force we had begun to build. There were more political struggles than those between the superpowers and between the first and third worlds. Divisiveness was spawned by the traditional political approaches to the problem. Sometimes controversies among the researchers and scientists made progress difficult. Many of them claimed to have the "correct analysis" upon which the political strategy for disarmament should be based.

The peace research movement emerged in Europe and the United States in the 1950s and 1960s. This movement made an important contribution toward our being in this place today. This happened in spite of such differences as those between the advocates of arms control and the advocates of disarmament.

Looking over the delegates, I picked out researchers I had known through the years. They devoted so much of their energies to the research and to bringing their findings to the attention of the political establishment. I remembered the way in which the peace research community had worked to increase the role of nongovernmental organizations in the U.N. deliberations on disarmament.

From the early 1980s researchers had begun to act as a kind of global lobby in the interest of humankind. They interacted with those who were operating from the traditional national-interest perspective. Surely it was this sophisticated and informed lobbying that convinced the practical politicians that policy could be made in "the human interest."[9]

The tenacious efforts of some of these researchers and other nongovernmental organizations in and around the United Nations had significantly changed the course of deliberations. The People's Security [10] lobby became an official delegation to the international meeting that drafted and was now bringing into force today's Treaty for General and Complete Disarmament.

Many nongovernmental organizations were represented by such official delegations to this signature ceremony.

As the People's Security delegation filed into the stand, observers jumped to their feet in a wild burst of applause. They represented more than anything else "our victory." It was a victory we knew to be possible only in the kind of game where everybody wins.

Among those we recognized in the delegation were the Japanese teacher from the Asian Regional ESR. The teacher was walking with African, Latin American and European educators whom we had elected to represent us at the ceremony. Walking among the International Physicians against Nuclear War[11] were a neurosurgeon from the Soviet Union and a psychiatrist from the United States.

The others I did not know. I assumed they were from social scientist, performing artist and other professional groups. These groups had begun to organize and build global networks for nuclear disarmament in the spring and summer of 1982. They had followed the example of the churches and the physicians, just as we had in forming Educators for Social Responsibility.

For a while I had believed the formal educational efforts had really made the difference, helping people to see the need to change. Educators had served as catalysts introducing peace studies into schools and all kinds of learning settings throughout the world. Work was developed since the early 1960s on the methods of teaching about alternatives to war and the possibilities for nonviolent conflict resolution. Eventually it began to be accepted even in some of the more conservative educational systems.[12]

Even now I was sure that education had been a very significant part of the movement toward this day of peace. Perhaps it was the most significant. The whole movement during the 1980s was an educative process in itself. People tried to learn. They struggled to instruct themselves in the issues related to weapons development, to national security, to ways of ending the arms race and to possible alternatives to war. It may have been one of the most important learning experiences in human history. We had learned about the international system. We came to know that our efforts to make our nations more secure through numerous and powerful arms only made us more insecure. That may have been the most important of all lessons. Yet cognitive learning, understanding even so important a phenomenon as armed insecurity, simply did not explain it all. Something more had made the difference.

Among the People's Security delegation I noted the U.S. senator who had been one of those to introduce the

Photo: UPI

Nuclear Freeze into the U.S. Senate. His presence there reminded me of the parallel development of education with political action. The citizens' movement had influenced and, in fact, provided the direction for changing political policies.

Yet I thought, too, of the nature of the early antinuclear efforts. The Nuclear Freeze, particularly, called for a halt to the way things were going and became a prelude to a new direction. The freeze, as it was first proposed and discussed, did not propose or contain a specific positive direction. Those positive energies I recalled from the cathedral service found a political vehicle when the antiwar movement joined the social justice movement.

The commitment to fulfilling human needs became as strong as the urgent desire to prevent human annihilation. That merger generated the really significant force. It kept us going through this past decade. It brought into the peace movement many who previously had not seen the problem of preventing nuclear annihilation and devising alternatives to war as their concern.

We began to see how these issues were inseparably related. It was like the way the feminists came to understand that the militaristic values propelling the arms race were the very same values that kept women "in their place." So, too, economically deprived and the political-

ly oppressed persons began to comprehend the war system as a fundamental cause of their condition.[13] Most people came to see that system pushing us closer and closer to the last day of civilization.

The connection to economic equity, social justice, and human rights gave us a very positive direction. The researchers had been putting out annual reports showing the social costs of the arms race from the mid-seventies on.[14] What helped us put things together were the budget cuts in human services coming at the same time as arms expenditures were increased incomprehensibly.

Anyone following world events was painfully aware of two significant trends. Severe economic crisis brought unemployment on a worldwide basis and global militarization increased. Many countries were falling under the control of the military. Virtually all were building large military establishments. Arms control negotiations were stalled as one technological "advance" after another produced ever deadlier weaponry. It took years before the need for an alternative international security system became clear to all.

The freeze and the proposals for cutting back on the big weapons helped to focus on the need for system change. That made more sweeping proposals possible. When the U.N. Second Special Session on Disarmament was convened in 1982, the general concern and growing fear brought it unprecedented public attention.

The event itself was no radical departure from the ordinary diplomatic trends and events. The opening session had the same atmosphere and the same procedures as on innumerable other sessions. On that day I sat in the section reserved for observers from nongovernmental organizations. I was excited and hopeful because the session was finally taking place. As I looked out at the assembly with so many close-cropped male heads and dark suits I thought, "It's all the same. How can anything different come out of this?"

I recalled that small core of hope, overlaid with the expectation that nothing would happen outside the established political order. It finally came to me. It was the environment in which the session took place. It was what was happening outside the halls that began to turn the tide.

It was the women, the religious community, the educators, the professionals, the researchers and those few politicians who began to understand. All of them reached out to take strength from each other. They acknowledged a belief in the possibility of a future. They affirmed that the human drama was not yet played out. That was what made the difference. People took responsibility for the future, recognizing that the structures in place were not adequate to the task.

So they took it up themselves with no small degree of fear but with courage and even joy. That was the real turning point. For me it was marked from the particular day when the largest of all the growing number of demonstrations for nuclear disarmament took place. It was a gesture of solidarity and support to the delegates of the Second Special Session on Disarmament.

Nearly a million people came from around the world to the streets of New York surrounding the United Nations and walked together to Central Park. The park that day was used for recreation, for celebration in a way in which it had never been before. Perhaps no public park had ever been used that way. The music, the speeches, and the cheers were the initiation of this very ritual we observe today.

As colorful as this crowd is, it pales in comparison with the crowd that took to the New York streets on June 12, 1982. Youngsters with the safety-pin earrings of the punk-rock generation and monks garbed in the robes of their religious orders moved together. Elderly persons and business executives in vests and ties walked side-by-side. Persons in wheelchairs and people pushing baby strollers joined the crowd. They had come from all over the world. The young and the old, those with means and those with none, to walk together. They said with one voice, "We will live! We choose life for ourselves and our children. And we will remember how close we are at this moment of choice to the possibility of death."

June 12, 1982, was the first day of hope. It was a day of affirmation. We knew there was the possibility that peace could be done because of our own commitment and that those who had risked and struggled before us. On a platform near the entrance to the park a group of Japanese musicians sat surrounded by banners carrying the slogan "Never Again." As we marched by, we took up that chant, "Never again! Never again!" We knew we had to remember. We had to remember Hiroshima, to remember the victims of weaponry and war and militarism.

Last fall when the discussions were being held about the place where today's ceremony should be held. Almost the only point on which everyone agreed was that the location should have profound significance to the commitment not to forget what we had done as well as what we almost did. It should be in one of the many places that now symbolize the dark side of ourselves. It should be one of those spots on earth where we came so close to destroying ourselves—Guernica, Auschwitz, Hiroshima, Nagasaki, Afghanistan, My Lai, Lebanon. It was finally decided that we would come to this stadium. We would observe that remembrance and this promise here in this place. We would come to this arena where the throats of poets were crushed and the hands of musicians were smashed. Here we would remember again the voices of those who cried for justice but were silenced by militarism. The militarism that was once so deaf to poetry and music, so fearful of justice, that it brought us close to the final silence and to losing the possibility of this beginning.

Reprinted by permission of Teachers College Record, Columbia University 525 W. 120th Street, New York, N.Y. 10027. Edited for this publication.

NOTES
1. Jonathan Schell, The Fate of the Earth (New York: Alfred A Knopf, 1982).
2. Educators for Social Responsibiility (Box 1711, New Rochelle, NY 10802), was founded in Brookline, Massachusetts, in 1981.
3. For information on this subject consult the U.N. Centre for Disarmament, United Nations, New York, NY 10017.
4. The text of the final document of SSDI is available from the U.N. Centre for Disarmament.
5. Information on the World Disarmament Campaign is also available from the U.N. Centre for Disarmament.
6. For description of such a system see Harry B. Hollins, "A Defensive Weapons System," The Bulletin of Atomic Scientists, June—July 1982. Offprints available from the Institute for World Order, 777 U.N. Plaza, New York, NY 10017.
7. Write to your denominational headquarters for a copy of your church's statements on peace and justice.
8. Nuclear Weapons Freeze Campaign Clearning House, 4144 Lindell Blvd, Suite 404, St. Louis, MO 63108.
9. Robert C. Johansen, *The National Interest and the Human Interest: An Analysis of US Foreign Policy* (Princeton, NJ: Princeton University Press, 1980.
10. For a definition of the concept of People's Security see Yoshikazu Sakamoto, "A Report of the Secretary General," *International Peace Research Association Newsletter*, Fall 1981.
11. Physicians for Social Responsibility, P.O. Box 411, Planetarium Station, New York, NY 10024.
12. Betty Reardon, *Militarization, Security and Peace Education* (Valley Forge, PA: United Ministries in Education, 1982).
13. Betty Reardon, "Militarism and Sexism: Influences on Education for War," *Connexion*, vol. 9, no. 3, Fall 1981.
14. Ruth Leger Sivard, *World Military and Social Expenditures* (Leesburg, VA: World Priorities, Inc.) (published annually since 1977).

VIGIL SONG

Chorus:

If you give me all your dreams
I'll give you all of mine
Too many dreamers are sleeping
And we're running out of time.

But if you give me all your hope
I'll give you all of mine.
If we hope together
We can make it through these times.

(Chorus)

And if you give me all your peace
I'll give you all of mine.
If we help each other
We can disarm ourselves in time.

(Chorus)

But if you give me all your voice
I'll give you all of mine.
We can sing together knowing
We can change these troubled times.

(Chorus)

Words by susan Savell © 1981 Used by permission. A filmstrip with record using this song is available from the Stewardship Council, United Church of Christ, 132 West 31 Street, New York, N.Y. 10001.

Hope for the Children

ST. CATHERINE 8. 8. 8. 8. 8. 8.
Henri F. Hemy 1864
Adapted by James G. Walton, 1874

Words by Douglas Clark, *1980

1. Hope for the chil-dren in our midst, Fac-ing a world that's con-flict torn; All that they ask is time to grow, And live the years for which they're born.

2. Ru-mors of war sound ev-'ry-where, Whis-per-ing there's no chance for peace. Yet for all chil-dren that we love, We will not yield till hate shall cease.

3. Peace is the goal of all we do; Love leads to jus-tice on the earth; Let jus-tice flow like wa-ter clear, So may we see the world's re-birth.

4. Hope for the chil-dren yet to be; Pray they may find years free from war. Let us make plow-shares of all swords, Har-vest-ing life healed ev-er more.

Hope for the chil-dren ev-'ry-where: We'll build for them a world of peace.

* With help from Polly Mattson. Used by permission.

JUSTICE IS SOMETHING WORTH FIGHTING FOR

by Robert Culver

In this piece and the two following, the necessity of war is described. Robert Culver bases his case on arguments and principles from the Bible. He lays out the reasonableness, even moral necessity, of certain wars. Connections are made between "limited war" and "just—or justified—war."

Culver states his respect for and disagreement with the "sturdy, sincere people of the peace churches." Political pacifism is held by Culver to be unrealistic.

The viewpoint given here is similar in many ways to that of the American Bishops' Pastoral. Comparisons between the statements might be interesting.

Culver is annual professor of theology at Winnipeg Theological Seminary, Manitoba, Canada. His book TOWARDS A BIBLICAL VIEW OF CIVIL GOVERNMENT, Moody Press, 1975, explains his views more fully. This article is taken from "Christianity Today," November 7, 1980, pp. 14-25, and is used by permission of Christianity Today, Inc., 465 Gundersen Drive, Carol Stream, Illinois 60187

Two illustrations of "just war" are included next. Both are explanations of why violence was believed necessary to bring justice in oppressive situations.

The first illustraion is excerpts from a book written by Kenneth David Kaunda, President of Zambia. The book KAUNDA ON VIOLENCE, edited by Colin M. Morris, tells in Kaunda's own words how he moved from being an advocate of Ghandian nonviolence to a violent response to what he considered to be injustice.

Photo: Craig Callan

The second example is the epilogue which is included in all four volumes of THE GOSPEL IN SOLENTINAME. The content of these volumes was gathered by Ernesto Cardenal and was first published in English in 1976 by Orbis Books. Cardenal was a Maryknoll priest sent with two others to work in Solentiname, islands on Lake Nicaragua. Each Sunday instead of a sermon, the priest and the people would talk together about the gospel for the day. The books report those conversations.

In this piece, Cardenal describes why young people of Solentiname took up arms. He is now minister of culture of Nicaragua.

These two illustrations are included because they point out the dilemma for those of us who advocate nonviolence and hold visions of peace which are based in justice. The ambiguity of that tension is painful. The struggle to be faithful is shown in the words used by these two men of faith from cultures which are very different than ours.

Christians of the second and third centuries living in the Roman Empire were almost unanimous in their opposition to war. Obedience to the gospel, so early church leaders argued, was consistent only with a position of nonresistance. Were their reasons adequate? Does their stand have doctrinal force for all ages?

Or may this rather be only a useful strategy for the believer under oppressive pagan government? Evangelicals today reject many views of the second and third centuries; the developing legalism, dependence on rites called sacraments for salvation (sacerdotalism), transfer of all liturgical acts and church government to a priestly class (prelacy). So we are surely free to reexamine early views on war.

Almost immediately after the Christians of the Empire received legal status the church leaders began to give the magistrates advice on how to conduct themselves in office. Of course, they included ideas on resorting to military force to govern their Empire, though the wars were, for so large an empire, largely internal. War had become mainly a policing action, to "keep the peace" of the Empire.

Against such a background, Ambrose of Milan, followed more adequately by Augustine of Hippo, formulated a doctrine for the use of coercive force by magistrates. Augustine, however, did not sit down and work out this view at one sitting. To discover it we must survey not only Book XIX of *City of God*, but 20 or more letters and tracts plus innumerable comments on biblical texts. Further, his statements were more practical than theoretical, lacking precise definition of governmental institutions, and so on. He was a man of a transitional period.

Many sincere young people have since personally passed through the same transition. Born in a milieu of what is called "nonresistance" (social and political separation), they have been forced by history to think through and act out a transition from it. Many of my generation — the one born during World War I and who fought World War II or supported it on the home front — did just that.

I was entering seminary when the newspaper headlines "War Is On," shocked us September 1, 1939. I had also read the headline, "Wall Street Crash" on October 1929. I have, therefore, vivid recollections of 10 years of worldwide economic depression and six years of worldwide war. Survival was the issue.

By 1941 when the draft began, I was forming my own opinions about the peace doctrine. By about 1946 it took the approximate form it still retains. Then, as now, I differed from several inherited opinions, which I nevertheless respect. When what we believe affects how others perceive us to be — bold, brave, cowardly, foolish, wise, consistent, inconsistent, orthodox, heterodox — caution and soft speaking become the order of the day; I wish to follow that order.

I am frequently among the sturdy, sincere people of the "peace" churches. I find rising in my heart a respect for their history of courage that often led to martyrdom. Somehow I then have small inclination to try to persuade them out of their beliefs. Their characteristic social isolation could never be universal for Christians. Many of them are now persuading themselves out of it. Yet seen from the inside it seems admirable.

With some reluctance, therefore, I come to details of my belief about war and the question of whether it is ever justifiable.

COME MARCH ALONG

Come march along and we'll sing a new song
Come salute the way of the dawning day
And death shall have no dominion here.
Though clouds grow dark and the sun disappears
Though the winds blow cold we shall rise to...

Call forth new children, new women and new men
Call forth new families, together we shall see
That death shall have no dominion here.
Though flames grow dark and hopes disappear
Though love blows cold we shall rise to...

Bring forth the tired and sick, the restless and the meek
Bring forth new warriors who care, to build the earth
And death shall have no dominion here.
Though times grow dark and vision disappears

Come march along and we'll sing a new song
Come salute the way of the dawning day
And death shall have no dominion here.

Song used by permission of the Institute of Cultural Affairs, 4750 North Sheridan Road, Chicago, Illinois, 60640.

OLD TESTAMENT

By any reasonable assessment, many divinely authorized (approved) wars, prosecuted wholly by God's people, are reported in the Old Testament. But what God prescribed in one dispensation he could forbid in another. One example is the eating of swine's flesh. What is more relevant is that contrary to common opinion, Old Testament believers lived under an ethical system in which any act of personal revenge was proscribed. Self-defense was permitted only with severe limitations. Kindness extended swiftly to one's neighbors — both compatriots and foreigners — was encouraged by Mosaic religion. What the priest and levite did in Jesus' Good Samaritan parable was contrary to Mosaism.

Passages like Romans 12:19-21 exude the very atmosphere of peace, but in this they are similar to Mosaic religion. Strack and Billerbeck, in their unique *Commentary on the New Testament Out of Talmud and Midrash*, provide seven pages of parallels from Old Testament and rabbinical sources. A large part of the passage is quoted directly from the Old Testament. For example, "But if thine enemy hunger, feed him; if he thirst, give him drink: for in so doing thou shalt heap coals of fire upon his head" is quoted from Proverbs 25:21-22.

King David was rebuked for even contemplating revenge on Nabal. Joab was executed by Solomon for an act of revenge. He shed the blood of war in time of peace. After Moses, the Jewish "citizen" had access to public law for justice, and if that failed he still did not have the right to take matters violently into his own hands, though self-defense against attack was not denied him. But use of physical force was limited even in defense of property — a proprietor could not slay a daylight burglar obviously bent on theft only. A nighttime burglar, whose intentions were not obvious, might be slain.

Thus, the Old Testament taught a personal ethic of nonretaliation and of nonviolence to neighbors, along with duties of kindness to all in need. It did not see this as contrary to its social ethic, which allowed limited personal self-defense, vigorous action against insurrection (Absalom), and just wars of defense and of execution of national policy. If these two strains of thought were consistent with one another in the Old Testament dispensation, might they not be consistent in the New Testament dispensation too? The answer seems to be yes.

SAYINGS OF JESUS

The principles of nonviolence to one's neighbor and nonresistance to evil, along with other ways of saying, "as much as lieth in you, live peaceably with all" (Romans 12:18), are certainly present in Jesus' words, especially in the Sermon on the Mount. Yet though none should deny that Jesus put moral ideals in a more purely spiritual perspective than Moses did, the break is not absolute, since after all, "Be ye holy, for I am holy" is Mosaic.

Moses made many statements about nonviolence in personal disputes, but he also set up a coercive civil structure for handling those disputes, though without encouraging excessive litigation. Jesus quoted Moses' law of exact public justice "an eye for an eye" and then put "resist not" the person that is "evil" (Matt. 5:39, RSV) beside it with an introductory, "but I say unto you." But he should not be understood as refusing all recourse to law when acts of persuasion fail. Nor should we think of him as merely forbidding physical retaliation; he is inculcating a deep spirit of love for God and humans. Paul prayed every day for Israel and could wish himself accursed from God if that would save them. More than once when the Jews tried to kill him, Paul ran.

But when they caught him he tried legal defense in Palestine. When that failed he appealed to Caesar. I think Paul knew what Jesus said about self-defense and recourse to law, and understood what Jesus meant. It is surely a mistake to interpret Jesus' sayings as if they must have unconditional application—that is, apart from other biblical revelation and apart from all interpretation.

Especially, attention must be given to hyperbole as a technique to capture attention and enforce a point. Jesus used it often. How else can we understand such a saying as: "If any…hateth not his own father, and mother, and wife, and children, and brethren and sisters, yea, and his own life also, he cannot be my disciple." (Luke 14:26) Jesus did not intend us to apply his sayings about lending, accompanying guests, presenting a cheek for smiting, and so on, without respect to common sense and a care for family and others who are neither borrowers or guests nor having temper tantrums.

The Old Testament is not wanting in instructions very similar to Jesus' famous sermon. Strack and Billerbeck provide sufficient evidence of parallels to one verse—Matt. 5:25, "agree with thine adversary quickly"—to cover most of three pages—and so on through the Sermon of the Mount. Jewish scholars rightly protest that Jesus' ethical sayings were not unique to him among ancient rabbis. Pacifist writers sometimes find what they think are their own pacifist teaching in the Old Testament, but when they do so the divinely commanded, not merely permitted, wars do not fit the scheme.

Jesus did not intend the literal, uninterpreted application of every one of these sayings. He did not even apply them to himself in this way. Though our perfect example of patience, when he was smitten on the face he answers, "If I have spoken evil bear witness of the evil: but if well, why smitest thou me?" (John 18:23, KJV) If we look only to the words, he did not obey his own precept for he did not turn the other cheek. Yet he had come to Jerusalem prepared not only to be smitten but crucified by those for whose forgiveness he would pray to God. (I am paraphrasing Augustine here.) He also gave some verbal defense. And though he once said, "Swear not at all," (Matt. 5:34, KJV) he testifies under oath at his own trial.

Likewise Paul seems to fail to obey his Savior, for when smitten on the face he cried out to the chief priest, "God shall smite thee, thou whited wall, for sittest thou to judge me after the law and commandest me to be smitten contrary to the law?" (Acts 23:3)

I am convinced those interpreters are correct who relate such precepts to the heart and the feelings. With mercy, love and grace we must act in intelligent kindness with regard to the true needs of people rather than simply giving them what they say they need. My father never turned away a hungry Indian in his life. We rented a farm on the Yakima reservation. But, he never granted demands for the very sources—horses, cattle, seed, tools—of his ability to pay his rent to the Indians. I think he met the true needs of these poor people and honored the intent of the Savior's words quite exactly. In return, the Indians respected him.

Two conclusions are suggested. First, the rigorous nonresistance to evil required by Anabaptist and modern pacifist interpretation is not required by Jesus. Neither is the rigorous nonparticipation in civic life—or social separation—so characteristic of Anabaptist sects. Second, the similarity of Jesus' ethic to the Mosaic ethic, enlarged upon by Old Testament poets and prophets, suggests that if Moses' disciples did not think they were required to embrace pacifism, probably Jesus' disciples need not embrace it either.

WAR: A MORAL EVIL?

Is it true that war, as such, is sin? War is a social evil; this cannot be denied. A disposition, national or personal, to glory in mortal combat is of the devil (James 4:1-2). War, however, is not an unmixed evil, or God would not have commanded wars to be initiated by his people. Furthermore, a sober view of history will find some good from settlement of international quarrels by war. It must be acknowledged, however, that most wars are both unnecessary and wrongfully motivated.

Yet Scripture never calls war, as such, a moral evil. Hell is an evil also, but it is a moral necessity. Evil lies behind the necessity for such things as hell, jails, criminal courts and war. Let us not be coerced from debate by unsupportable, question-begging denunciations. If war were morally evil, per se, we would not read of Michael and his holy angels at war with the devil and his angels. (Rev. 12:7) The military figures and symbols of Scripture would be inappropriate. Certainly no text of the Bible would declare, "The Lord is a man of war, Jehovah is his name." (Exod. 15:3, KJV) After all, Miriam was a prophetess.

Most biblically motivated pacifists agree that the sword has been given to rulers of civil commonwealths. Scripture certainly says so—whether the civil unit be small or large. It is not correct to say, as one contemporary pacifist writer does, that Romans 13 is only descriptive of what happens *wrongly* in this world. Good persons must regard obedience to the magistrate and approving respect for the magistrate's sword as a matter of conscience (v.5).

If it is right for rulers to use coercive force, then most persons of good will and good conscience will say that it is right for the Christian to be a part of the force. Reality, most will agree, provides no "division of labor" whereby one section of humanity, as a matter of necessity and duty, does something for my benefit in which it is too sinful for me to help out. How can I be excused from that task by making contribution to society in some other way? It is of great significance that military duty in the Mosaic system was not restricted to a military class and that executions by stoning were carried out by the whole congregation of Israel.

SOCIAL ISOLATION

There really appears to be no way in this world to escape complicity, or, as some would have it, cooperation, in the ongoing of necessary social processes and institutions: "For this cause pay ye tribute also." (Romans 13:6) Membership in family, clan, nation, tribe, or whatever is a "given." We simply cannot escape it. This is a demonstrably scriptural teaching. Long chapters in good books by eminent Christian authors treat this with learning and reverent piety. It is simply impossible for earth-and-time-bound humans to step out of the world—family, tribe, clan, nation—to make their "contributions." Social separation is not a goal to be striven for. We are supposed to do our service for God in society, not out of it or beside it. True, sometimes within that family, tribe, clan, or nation my Christian witness may lead to suffering. If it is to be thought "not strange," neither is it to be contrived. (see I Peter 3:12-19) Sometimes, of course, social ostracism makes social separation necessary.

It has been pointed out by Werner Elert in *The Christian Ethos* that there is no consistency in the refusal to be a part of civil government, refusal even to endorse its task of restraining evil men, unless one goes beyond the Mennonite position to Tolstoy's: To fight evil is sin; because the state fights against evil, the state itself is evil. Recent *avant garde* pacifists like to accomplish the same end by a bit of verbal magic. Drop the neutral word "force" and employ instead the pejorative word "violence." In this way the murderer employs violence to kill men and the policeman uses violence to apprehend and to restrain the murderer. The murderer and the policeman are equally evil. Such a view is perverse and certainly merits the biblical denunciation of those who call evil good, good evil, and who put darkness for light and light for darkness. (Isa. 5:20)

JUST WAR: A BIBLICAL BASE

What then is the Christian witness to "the state" in regard to war? Certainly no professor or prelate has professional competence to give omniscient guidance. Everywhere, for us as it was for Paul, government is a universal fact in a world under the condition of sin. Paul and other New Testament Christians did not tell the pagan governments much of anything. But once the ancient Roman Empire officially professed Christianity, Christian teachers had considerable to say.

When people in civil authority will listen, Christianity speaks. Yet we search in vain for any adequate, timeless statement of the "doctrine of the justified war." There have been many doctrines of the just war. In my judgment, God-fearing Christians and their counselors in every age, in dealing with this problem have applied rather constant conceptions of basic biblical truth coupled with their best spiritual insights and common sense. Ancient Christians knew they could not be part of Caesar's army if Caesar were to compel them to worship an image of the emperor. Soviet Christians are in the same position if compelled to sign an atheistic oath upon induction into the army. Yet either group might be quite willing to serve in a national army if overt denial of their faith were not required. Each might subscribe to some sort of just war theory if given a chance. There is a praiseworthy sameness through the centuries in spite of apparent differences.

The sameness has roots in a common biblical world view. This is essentially one through all the ages. The biblical God is Creator, Sustainer and providential Ruler over and in a world where sin and the Devil also "reign." Christians of every epoch know that humans are sinners and incorrigibly rebellious. They must be coerced to good behavior by others who are likewise sinners and rebellious. Yet it is right that these rulers employ police, backed up by courts, prisons, guillotine, and gallows and, if national policy requires it, by army, navy, draft law, and much, if not all, of the rest. This puts Christians on the side of their magistrates and civil order except in the very most unusual of situations. They recognize that short of the consummation there is no alternative. The system works imperfectly, but civilization goes on. These Christians have also read I Timothy 2:1-4 and so pray for their rulers. Ordinarily Christians support and obey them in both war and peace. Christians as well as other subjects have expected their rulers to be foresighted in protecting their realms, having information about dangerous attacks and making preparation for them before they occur. They have not usually tried to tell their rulers when or how they ought or ought not to do these things.

It is a reasonable assumption most of the time that our full-time rulers are rational and in possession of facts they cannot disclose to the public. Assumptions to the contrary—now seemingly universal in democratic countries—are hardly verifiable, much as we wish our leaders would individually consult us about every next move. It is also commonly assumed in Christendom that no army should wantonly attack nonmilitary targets or harm noncombatants, especially women, children and the aged.

These are some of the notions associated with Christian sentiment and dignified by the term "just war theory." They have been given much more than lip service, with the result that for centuries Europe's wars were restrained in their devastations. Since the U.S. Civil War and especially the bombings of Dresden, Germany, and England's cities in World War II, and the fearful climax of that war in the annihilation of Hiroshima and Nagasaki, the outlook has changed. Even so, "saturation bombing" has not won the moral approval of military people everywhere, and talk of "total" war is, I think, still just that—talk. It has more affinity with journalistic and theoretical superspeak than with any leading nation's serious policy. I do not think it can be demonstrated that wars involve all of a nation's people and resources now any more than in ancient times. Consider some of the tribal wars in the Book of Judges.

AUGUSTINE'S VIEW

It is strange that Augustine should be credited with first giving currency to the "just war" idea. In his view none of the works of humankind are just—that is righteous.

Augustine's judgment on human beings, based largely on Paul's epistles, was that they are without exception sinful, lost, unable even to seek a way to God. Men and women individually and collectively are corrupt.

So first, this teaching cannot be a formula for initiating, supporting, or conducting a simon-pure righteous war with no moral ambiguity. Sin manages to pervade all things human. Even theological faculties exist under the condition of sin. In this sense there is no just Christian missionary society or evangelistic campaign. Pride and selfishness vitiate all persons and all their works.

By comparing passages from several of his writings,

scholars have determined that Augustine's idea of a justified war would be a war to defend justice. It would be motivated by love even for the enemy—I do not know how a government loves anything—and would be conducted without unnecessary violence. Most important, war must be waged only by the authority of rulers, not of private persons.

These rules, with some added notions, prevailed through medieval times. As we have seen earlier, the 16th century Reformers acknowledged the same, yet all leaned away from war as a way of protecting their rights. All seem to have acknowledged the right—even duty— of rulers to wage war on necessary occasions. They did not, however, any more than Augustine, expect from them very much righteousness, either in war or peace.

It is impossible to trace here the changing definitions of "just war" as they have evolved in the present century. Even what goes now for "nuclear pacifism"—that the results of any unlimited warfare in destruction of the race make all wars immoral—is, according to Paul Ramsey, a rather extreme form of just war theory.

Without trying to recite the post-World War II, 35-year-old debate, many Catholics and Protestants seem to be saying something like this: Modern scientific methods and weapons have given nations the power to obliterate one another as nations. This frightful prospect, however, is not entirely new. The Assyrians, for instance, practiced a kind of obliteration warfare in a large part of their area of the ancient Orient.

Today we hear the term "limited war" as well as "just war." The concepts are closely related. There is biblical support for a limited war doctrine. The special case of annihilation of the Canaanites, Midianites, and others in the initial conquest of the Promised Land may cause us to forget that ordinarily the Old Testament put limits on allowable destructive force in any war. Consider the prophet Amos. In his first two chapters, five neighbors of Israel and Judah are cited for divine judgment. The causes in each case involve flagrant breaches of what today might be called a civilized code of war. For instance, Damascus had been unnecessarily brutal against Gileadite civilians in a war raid. (Amos 1:3) Gaza had unnecessarily dispossessed a whole people of their territory (Amos 1:6) Moab had committed sacrilege by wantonly desecrating the national cemetery of the kingdom of Edom. No previous word of Scripture addressed these heathen nations on the subject of civilized conduct of war. These standards must be assigned to natural light, or natural law. These passages in Amos tacitly assume a doctrine of limited (just) war.

Since atomic power and other more potent powers are here, it is to be expected that nations will use them. The nuclear and atomic "club" gains new members frequently. Yet we now know that to rely solely on these super weapons renders a nation unable successfully to wage war on lesser levels, and turns loose all sorts of insurgencies, coups, and adventurism among the violence-prone of the world.

If the present civilized order is to continue, rulers "of good will" must control the effective weapons their moral standards permit them to use. A missile possessed and aimed at Leningrad's residential district will likely never be used; one aimed at a munitions depot in Russia could be and might be used by men of conscience. The principle of limited war is the same as traditional just war theory. The problems of the nuclear age are no different in principle from any previous age. In a world that never can eliminate war, limited—that is, *justly-waged-war*—is more important than ever before. To propose that instead we insist on political pacifism, abandonment of war as an instrument of national policy, is utterly unrealistic. If we deny any nation the right of justified war we condemn it to destruction by those with no moral scruples at all.

In conclusion, we must remember that Jesus pronounced the peacemakers blessed. Some think the peacemakers are all employed at work like producing crops, running factories and schools, perhaps bandaging wounds, preaching sermons, and soothing irritated tempers. People in these endeavors do employ some of the arts of peacemaking. But they are not the whole of the peacemaking enterprise. Some of the peacemakers win military campaigns decisively enough and with sufficient justice that no one cares to challenge the civil order for a long time. I prefer to think that Jesus meant to include *all* peacemakers.

(Unless otherwise noted, Scriptures quoted in the article are from the the King James Version.)

FROM ZAMBIA—KAUNDA ON VIOLENCE

by Colin M. Morris
(An Excerpt)

The jacket for Kaunda's book uses these words to describe its contents:

No world statesmen since Mahatma Gandhi has been so passionate an advocate of nonviolence as Kenneth David Kaunda, President of Zambia. He used with great effect the tactics of passive resistance against the British in his country's freedom struggle.

But in the first year of Zambia's life, Ian Smith's government in neighboring Rhodesia declared illegal independence. There began a long and bitter struggle for majority rule, with Zambia becoming increasingly embroiled as a guerrilla base, a sanctuary for refugees, victim as well as supporter of U.N. economic sanctions against Rhodesia and as a target for Rhodesian air and land strikes.

As one attempt after another at getting a constitutional settlement failed, Kaunda found the tension between his belief in nonviolence and his passion for justice in Rhodesia intolerable. He was forced to abandon the attitudes of a lifetime and accept the inevitability of armed struggle. He gives his reasons with utmost frankness. In Kaunda's own words:

Regrettably, my experience does not allow me to believe that evil left unchecked eventually defeats itself—you either fight it or feed it, and each of these alternatives involves getting your hands dirty. To allow the Nazis to

Photo: UN/Y. Nagata

rule the world would have been to connive with evil; but to overthrow them by war was also to traffic in evil. And those were the only alternatives. There was no idealistic middle way.

The test for such terrible times as these is not 'He that lives by the sword will perish by it' but 'There is none righteous, not one....' If that is true then we are in the miserable business of having to judge different forms of evil by marginal percentages. That is what statesmanship is all about underneath the pomp and circumstances—knife-edge judgments that one course of action will be slightly less harmful than another. To canvas a guiltless third way as the pacifist does is to risk irrelevance.

I know this—having prayed and pleaded and waited for the whites in Rhodesia to awaken from their sleep and see what terrible things they were doing to their black fellow-citizens and neighbors in the name of so-called civilization. Sadly, it was not the murmur of sweet reason but the sound of gunfire which alerted them to the hour of judgment.

I enter only this special plea for some kind of discrimination to be made in judging those who do acts of violence. The rich and powerful have a wide variety of weapons at their disposal which are denied to the poor. The violence of the underdog is strident, crude and obvious. The violence of the top-dog is often subtle and invisible. It spans a range which takes in international economic pressures, control of the media, manipulation of the educational system and psychological conditioning, as well as the more visible strong-arm methods.

It is this gigantic spider's web of interlocking systems that the poor and the black and the helpless are up against. So they have the right to ask that the world is alert to the secret violence which is exerted against them long before they actually retaliate in anger. When the first stone is thrown and the original barricade is stormed that is not the primary move in the game.

The truth is not so simple as the usual propaganda ploy tries to suggest—that black or communist or anarchist or nationalist or tribal agitators are disturbing an otherwise peaceful society. The peace was broken long before the first signs of disturbance reached the surface. The underdogs demand only this special consideration from the judges in the tribunals at which their desperate actions are weighed—not that they be given any favored treatment because they are black or poor or voiceless, but that the true magnitude of the forms of violence which can be applied against them because they are black and poor and voiceless be taken fully into account.

I ended up supporting armed struggle in Zimbabwe because I could no longer believe that ANYTHING is preferable to the use of force. I have been much taken with some words of a Victorian writer, Douglas Jerrold: "...not peace at any price. There is a peace more destructive to the personhood of a living human than war is destructive of his body. Chains are worse than bayonets."

Yes, if one must make that terrible choice, I do believe that chains are worse than bayonets. We never had the luxury of choosing between the strategies of perfection and those of harsh realism. We never had any option but to weigh up one form of evil against another and ask for God's forgiveness as we undertook to do what had to be done.

Or at least we did have one other option, and this is the final ironic twist to the saga of the Unilateral Declaration of Independence. I still believe that had Britain been prepared to risk a limited degree of force at the outset Britain might have achieved a just peace. But for whatever reasons Britain chose the way of misguided pacifism and made years of civil war inevitable.

....What is at stake in South Africa, and also Namibia, is simply humankind's right to be human—and that cannot be negotiable in return for supplies of uranium and precious metals, favorable terms of trade or even the chance to play against an excellent rugby team. APARTHEID'S challenge not only to Africa but to all humanity is so absolute that if there is no other way we must face up, as the free world has done before in this century, to a long, hard struggle which cannot exclude the use of force. Pray God we may all be preserved from such an awful fate.

Only South Africa itself has the power to avert what is rapidly becoming inevitable by demolishing the whole vicious apparatus of APARTHEID, setting all South Africa's peoples free from captivity to the past and offering their immense talents and energy in the service of the development of the whole continent. I am not optimistic, but I have much faith in the providence of God. That alone seems to stand between us and the void.

Used by permission of Collins Publishers

JOURNEY ON

(Can be sung to the tune: "From Elcho Island")

Journey on, journey on, all humankind,
Future is waiting for you.
Struggling, stumbling, all of life through,
Future is waiting for you.

(hum the tune)

Opportunities, opportunities, all in your hand,
Our minds are limited to foretell.
All of our own, and nature of unseen,
Future is waiting for you.

(hum the tune)

Journey on, journey on, all humankind,
Future is waiting for you.

Song used by permission of the Institute of Cultural Affairs, 4750 North Sheridan Road, Chicago, Illinois, 60640.

FROM NICARAGUA—EPILOGUE OF "THE GOSPEL IN SOLENTINAME"

by Ernesto Cardenal

Twelve years ago I arrived at Solentiname with two companions to found a small, contemplative community. Contemplation means union with God. We soon became aware that this union with God brought us before all else into union with the common workers, very poor and very abandoned, who lived dispersed along the shores of the archipelago.

Contemplation also brought us to the revolution. It had to be that way. If not, it would have been fake contemplation. My old novice master, Thomas Merton, the inspirer and spiritual director of our foundation, told me that in Latin America I could not separate myself from political strife.

In the beginning we would have preferred a revolution with nonviolent methods. But we soon began to realize that at this time in Nicaragua a nonviolent struggle is not feasible. Even Gandhi would agree with us. The truth is that all authentic revolutionaries prefer nonviolence to violence; but they are not always free to choose.

The Gospel was what most radicalized us politically. Every Sunday in Mass we discussed the Gospel in a dialogue with the common people. With admirable simplicity and profound theology, they began to understand the core of the Gospel message: The announcement of the New Age of God, that is, the establishment on this earth of a just society, without exploiters or exploited, with all goods in common, just like the society in which the first Christians lived. But above all else the Gospel taught us that the word of God is not only to be heard, but also to be put into practice.

As the common people of Solentiname got deeper and deeper into the Gospel, they could not help but feel united to their brothers and sisters who were suffering persecution and terror, who were imprisoned, tortured, murdered; they were violated and their homes were burnt. They also felt solidarity with all who with compassion for their neighbor were offering their lives. For this solidarity to be real, they had to lay security, and life, on the line.

In Solentiname it was well known that we were not going to enjoy peace and tranquility if we wanted to put into practice the word of God. We knew that the hour of sacrifice was going to arrive. This hour has now come. Now in our community everything is over.

There a school of primitive painting became famous throughout the world. Paintings, woodwork, and various handicrafts from Solentiname are sold not only in Managua, but also in New York, Washington, Paris, Venezuela, Puerto Rico, Switzerland, and Germany. Lately common workers from Solentiname had begun to write beautiful poetry. Their poems were published in Nicaragua and other countries.

Several films were made in Solentiname, one of them by BBC in London. Much has been written about Solentiname in various languages; records have been made, even in German. We have in that distant corner of the lake a great library gathered during a lifetime. We had a collection of pre-Columbian art found in Solentiname that grew through the years. We had a large guest house with plenty of beds for visitors. We had ovens for ceramics and a large shop for all kinds of handicrafts. There we worked with wood, leather, copper, bronze, and silver. We were also developing communal work for young persons through a cooperative.

The cooperative, with the help of a German institution, was about ready to begin a dairy and factory of European-style cheese. It was said in Germany: "Solentiname is everywhere, it is the beginning of a more human world. It is a Christian life — not just waiting for a better world, but working for their neighbor's peace, for peace in nature, for peace within the community." In Venezuela it was said that "Solentiname is something so God-like and so much of this world that it is a place where poetry, painting, and the harvest do not divide people into poets and farmers, but constitute the solidarity of one life." Now all that is over.

Twelve years ago, when the apostolic nuncio approved my project to found a new monastery, he told me that he preferred that the community be established in a less remote place than Solentiname, because there we would have no visitors. The truth is that we were always flooded with visitors from Nicaragua and other countries. Many times they were people who arrived in Nicaragua only to visit Solentiname; sometimes they arrived directly by way of Los Chiles or San Carlos, without any interest in even visiting Managua. Abundant correspondence from all parts of the world arrived in Solentiname.

But now brush will grow once again where our community used to be, just as it did before our arrival. There, there was a workers' mass, there were paintings, statues, books, records, classes, smiles of beautiful children, poetry, song. Now all that is left is the savage beauty of nature. I lived a very happy life in that near paradise that was Solentiname. But I was always ready to sacrifice it all. And now we have.

One day it happened that a group of boys and girls from Solentiname, because of profound convictions and after having let it mature for a long time, decided to take up arms. Why did they do it? They did it for only one reason: for their love for the New Age of God, for the ardent desire that a just society be implanted, a real and concrete New Age of God here on earth. When the time came, these boys and girls fought with great valor, but they also fought as Christians. That morning at San Carlos, they tried several times with a loudspeaker to reason with the guards so they might not have to fire a single shot. But the guards responded to their reasoning with submachine gunfire. With great regret, they also were forced to shoot.

Alejandro Guevara, one of those from my community, entered the building when in it there were no longer any but dead or wounded soldiers. He was going to set fire to it so that there would be no doubt about the success of the assault, but out of consideration for the wounded, he did not do it. Because the building was not burned, it was officially denied that it was taken.

I congratulate myself that these young Christians fought without hate — above all, without hate for the wounded guards, poor persons like themselves, also exploited. It is horrible that there are dead and wounded. We wish that there were not a struggle in Nicaragua, but this does not depend upon the oppressed people that are only defending themselves.

Some day there will be no more war in Nicaragua, no more guards, who are common people killing other common people. Instead there will be an abundance of schools, hospitals, and clinics for everyone, food adequate for everyone, art and entertainment. But most important, there will be love among all.

Now the repression that has gone on so long in the North has arrived in Solentiname. A tremendous number of the common people have had to flee, others are in exile, remembering those beautiful islands with their now destroyed homes. They would be there yet, living tranquil lives, dedicated to their daily tasks. But they thought of their neighbor, and of Nicaragua, and began to work for them.

I do not think about the reconstruction of our small community of Solentiname. I think of a task much more important that we all have — the reconstruction of the whole country.

EPILOGUE of "The Gospel in Solentiname" by Ernesto Cardenal, Orbis Books, Maryknoll, NY 10545 In October 1977, during a period of countrywide upheaval, the Nicaraguan National Guard ravaged the Solentiname community. In December, writing from Costa Rica, Cardenal explained in a "Letter to the People of Nicaragua" why he has joined the Sandinista guerrillas. The above translation by William Barbieri is reprinted with permission of the National Catholic Reporter, Box 281, Kansas City, Missouri, 64141. It has been edited for this publication.

Peace

The earth is Peace
The heart of the earth is Peace
Greater than the sky
Bluer than the ocean
Hotter than the sun
The heart of the earth is Peace
Kissing the earth
The soles of my feet feel unworthy
Absorbing everything
The earth brings grass and flowers
The soles of my feet feel unworthy

It is neither bow, nor sword, nor spear
Nor machine guns, cannons, tanks
The problem is nuclear weapons
and electronic weapons
The soles of my feet are angry
At the hands which make those weapons
At the fingers which pry and twist the buttons
The hungry children are crying
In the shadow of this great humanity
The soles of my feet pain and hurt

It is neither bow nor sword nor spear
Nor machine gun, cannon, tank
Nor nuclear weapons, electronic weapons
The problem is Peace
One is Peace
Two is Peace
Three is Peace
It is the heart of God
Saddened by Peace being pushed out
Of the Milky Way and the Star Clouds
It is the heart of God
Wishing fervently for Peace
Stepping on this fiery hot earth
The soles of my feet are burning
Stepping on this blazing earth
The soles of my feet are burning
and my body
The burning sacrifice

by Rev. Moon Ik-hwan

Excerpted from THE WISH, by Lee Sun-ai and Don Luce, Friendship Press © 1984.

PART TWO: WORKING THAT PEACE MAY COME

In Part One, various visions of peace were described. None of these visions become reality simply by being stated. Action and commitment is necessary for visions to become more than mere possibilities.

In this section, a variety of actions are described. It is unlikely that all the actions will seem appropriate to you and those who share your vision of a peaceful world. It is hoped that sharing these actions will stimulate you to plan ways in which your vision can be lived out.

Forms of action in this section include:
—education toward peace for children and youth

—disarmament campaigns in Canada
—action by youth in the church in the German Democratic Republic (East Germany)
—a letter from Tolstoy written in 1899 to a young man facing the draft into the peacetime Hessian army
—a form of tax protest
—a foreign-born woman's action toward a referendum sponsored by Jobs with Peace—the history of which is described—asking for transfer of some funds from military to social purposes.

Photo: UPI

41

We Shall Overcome

Traditional

1 We shall o - ver - come,___ We shall o - ver - come,___
2 We're on to vic - to - ry,___ We're on to vic - to - ry,___
3 We'll walk hand in hand,___ We'll walk hand in hand,___
4 The truth shall make us free,___ The truth shall make us free,___

We shall o - ver - come some day.___
We're on to vic - to - ry some day.___
We'll walk hand in hand some day.___
The truth shall make us free some day.___

Oh,___ deep in my

heart, I do be - lieve,

We shall o - ver - come some day.
We're on to vic - to - ry some day.
We'll walk hand in hand some day.
The truth shall make us free some day.

Shalom Chaverim

Paul Abels (English words)

Israeli round

Sha - lom, cha - ve - rim! Sha - lom, cha - ve - rim! Sha - lom, sha - lom!
Sha - lom, my friends! Sha - lom, my friends! Sha - lom, sha - lom!

Le - hit ra - ot. Le - hit ra - ot. Sha - lom, sha - lom!
We'll see you a - gain. We'll see you a - gain. Sha - lom, sha - lom!

THAT CHILDREN MAY COME TO KNOW AND LOVE PEACE: AGE LEVEL GUIDELINES FOR PEACE EDUCATION

A song from the musical *South Pacific* says that we have to carefully taught to hate. The North American culture, particularly in the United States, has ingredients in it which teach people to love war rather than peace. Our society is full of militaristic values—competition, winning, individualism—which the children learn from society by living here.

To bring to reality the biblical vision of peace, Shalom, people are needed who…

…understand that love means a concern for justice and who therefore seek to work toward a society and world in which all people have what they need for a fully human existence.

…are well informed and understand the complexity of social and political issues but who nevertheless can commit themselves to a course of action.

…seek dialogue with different points of view and who are prepared to seek to understand the viewpoints of others.

…are humble and know the depth of their own brokenness, or sinfulness, in their personal relationships and in their participation in social and economic systems.

…can challenge all that block and destroy God's Shalom—but still forgive those who hurt them.

…seek and are open to both the support and the challenge that comes from a community of faith and through a life of prayer and meditation.

These personal characteristics of people of peace were identified by "Shalom Education: An Ecumenical Task Force on Christian Education for World Peace." The task force is a Chicago-based group which finds and creates resource materials to provide Christian education programs with methods, values and perspectives that will teach the way of peace, called by the group "the vision of Shalom."

Among the resources created by the Shalom education group is a small booklet of age-level guidelines for education toward Shalom. In that booklet, six qualities or perspectives are given as the structure for all education levels:

1. Understanding the biblical vision of Shalom
2. Valuing all people
3. Participating in creative change
4. Using conflict creatively
5. Caring for and sharing world resources
6. Choosing to live by the vision of Shalom

Included here are those guidelines for education of children and youth. The guidelines suggest how the development of these qualities and perspectives can be fostered according to the developmental characteristics of each age group.

The guidelines include different life-responses which children of those ages may make. Because humans develop in different ways and to varying points of maturity, the suggestions may not "fit" for every person in every age group. Ideas suggested might be used with people just younger or older than the specified age.

Most of the items listed describe what experiences curriculum might include. Many relate to what could happen in homes as well as formal education settings. Usually they are in terms of what the teacher, leader or adult will do to help participants in the learning experience develop the desired quality or perspective. Statements in quotation marks are ones which the person of the age group might make or they may be patterns for statements by leaders, teachers or adults.

The are adapted from *Teaching Toward a Faithful Vision: Participant's Manual*, pp. 11-16. Copyright ©1977 by Discipleship Resources.

INFANTS TO FOUR-YEAR-OLDS

Little children tend to develop best in dependable, stable relationships in which those in authority consistently reflect Shalom values. Children need to experience the world as a safe and dependable place. In these early years, they are developing the crucial basis for living the Shalom vision. When effective communication has been established, repetition of it as a ritual is valuable and enjoyable for children.

1. Understanding the biblical vision of Shalom

Show children what Shalom is through people who "live out" the Shalom vision in their loving and just relationships with children and with each other.

2. Valuing all people

a. Affirm the worth of all people. "I am a special person even though I am little. Susie is special, too." One person's importance is not diminished by another's. "Daddy and Mommy love all of us."

b. Help children develop positive attitudes toward differences among people and cultures. "It's fun to know different kinds of people."

3. Participating in creative change

Help children feel supported in exploring, investigating, and trying new experiences. "It is fun to try new things."

4. Using conflict creatively

Help children understand that everyone experiences strong feelings. Emotions are okay—a part of God's plan. "Sometimes I get angry."

5. Caring for and sharing world resources

a. Help children enjoy the natural world. "I like the farm! I like the plants growing here!"

b. Develop responsibility, stewardship. "Let's not litter. Let's clean up our mess."

6. Chosing to live by the Shalom vision

a. Foster self-esteem. "I can do it!"

b. Facilitate children's participation in a caring community. "Carol and Rich really like me." "I can make friends."

Photo: J.R. Compton

KINDERGARTEN CHILDREN

Children of this age identify authority and power with bigness. So they may see bigger things as better. Adults can reinforce a child's sense of worth by making it clear that often small things, like children, have special value. Children at this age also begin to move from concerns of reward and punishment to understanding simple exchange of favors. So concentrate on the idea of "fairness" and develop skills of sharing and cooperation. Reflecting the Shalom vision in our own relationships and life-style is our most important "teaching tool."

1. Understanding the biblical vision of Shalom

a. Affirm that God works through people.

b. Show that taking care of animals and plant life is part of God's plan for us.

c. Include words about Shalom, peace and justice even though the concepts will not be fully understood until later.

2. Valuing all people

a. Help children explore through stories and art how people make us feel "special"; celebrate this as part of God's love for us.

b. Affirm the worth of all people. "The person who does the cleaning is as important as the doctor."

c. Help children recognize and appreciate similarities. "Everyone needs love and someone to love." "Everybody must have food."

d. Help children deal with reality. Some people are treated as worthless on television – "I don't know anyone who is all bad like that man. People are usually both good and bad."

e. Help children develop positive attitudes toward differences among peoples, cultures, generations. "Lynn's grandfather is a good friend to have."

f. Expose children to a variety of ethnic, religious and sex roles, avoiding those which stereotype or demean people.

3. Participating in creative change

a. Expand the sense of fairness by reminding children of the need to exchange favors. "Let's ask David to play. Then when we want to play, he will ask us to play, too."

b. Promote understanding of realities that *cannot* be changed. "Your sister will always be older."

c. Focus attention on situations that *can be* changed. "You can ask for help." "What do you want to do about this?"

d. Build awareness of rights of others. "Each one gets a turn."

e. Raise consciousness about greed, hunger, over-consumption and materialism by discussing and getting involved in projects of recycling toys and clothes, making or repairing things as alternatives to buying *new things*.

4. Using conflict creatively

a. Teach techniques for conflict resolution. "You are old enough to manage this yourself." "You can *talk with her about it* and solve it if you try."

b. Help children deal with the devastating effect of television violence. "I don't like this story. It's too mean." Help children relate this violence to injuries and hurts of people and animals they care for.

5. Caring for and sharing world resources

a. Develop responsibility, stewardship. "Let's throw this trash in the wastebasket. If this were my house, I'd want to keep it clean."

b. Counteract the persistent pull toward increasing materialism by television commercials, giveaway shows, contests, etc. "We can have fun without having 'first place' or 'all mine.'"

c. Provide models of a responsible style of consumption. "I drive a small car because we need to use less gas."

6. Choosing to live by the Shalom vision

a. Foster self-esteem. "You can do it." "All people get mad. It's OKAY to feel that way but it isn't OKAY to hurt someone else."

b. Develop respect for our physical bodies. "My body is a wonderful thing. I take care of it."

c. Enable children to grow in self-discipline. "I want the ball now, but I'll wait for my turn."

d. Develop a concept of forgiveness. "Sally lost the ball but she didn't mean to."

e. Foster a spirit of community. "Let's play together." Talk about why we need rules.

f. Promote a sense of human responsibility for the affairs of the world. "Our family is sending money to feed refugees."

g. Encourage actions on behalf of people around the world, using concrete realities, perhaps pictures of people helping others.

h. Develop a sense of respect for animals, plants, the non-organic. "Plants need food and water just like we do."

FIRST AND SECOND GRADES

At this age, children are still egocentric and only beginning to empathize with others. They begin to sort out differences between fantasy and reality. So story telling is a tool for broadening their world to include people different from them. Stories can also encourage the child's sense of "fairness" as part of Shalom.

1. Understanding the biblical vision of Shalom
a. Use portions of the Bible that teach the vision.
b. Make the values of Shalom an integral part of the child's life rather than just words.
c. Sing songs about peacemakers and peace.

2. Valuing all people
a. Have children play-act Jesus' love of differences constructively and *affirmatively,* while pointing out similarities in people everywhere.

3. Participating in creative change
a. Intentionally include the values of freedom, justice and dignity for all.
b. Discuss the major rules in class or home to develop an understanding of authority as more than just power. "Why do we have this rule? What would happen if we didn't?"
c. Plan activities that build a sense of belonging.
d. Expand feelings of belonging beyond family to the class and community. Take a field trip to the city boundaries and talk about how we need each other in the community.

4. Using conflict creatively
a. Create a family or classroom climate that provides opportunities for children to acknowledge and work through conflicts, including beneath the surface.
b. Expect negative feelings and conflicts; deal with them creatively through drama, art, music, brief conversations and stories.
c. Foster respect for the human body. As children grow in their love and respect for their own bodies, they will grow in love and respect for others and will not want to kill.
d. Avoid the use of military figures as "models."
e. Use Bible stories such as Joseph dealing with his brothers to discuss interpersonal conflict. "Was he fair? Why? Why not?"

5. Caring for and sharing world resources
a. Give high priority to the responsible use of the world's resources.
b. Help children to live in harmony with people and nature.
c. Talk about poverty as having several causes. "Some people are greedy. Some are careless and wasteful. Some live where there aren't any jobs." Help children choose one part of the problem on which to work (having a puppet show on greed, participating in a special money raising project)

6. Choosing to live by the Shalom vision
a. Affirm self-esteem.
b. Heighten responsible decision-making. Teach children to question "Why?" and guide them in making decisions in their daily actions. Help them to understand how their decisions affect their lives and those of others near and far.
c. Address value and life style issues by modeling "Shalom-like" behavior. "Let's not use paper plates so we don't waste more trees and help keep our world whole."
d. Stress empathy that can result in sharing rather than paternalism. "If we all share, then no one has to worry about having enough." The concept of service to others should go beyond the idea of just donors and recipients.

Photo: David Strickler

THIRD AND FOURTH GRADERS

Developmentally, no sharp differences divide those in first and second grade from those in third and fourth grade. So the suggestions made above apply here too with a special emphasis on clarifying concepts of justice, responsibility and fairness. Stories are still a powerful tool and may begin to include real people who are heroes and heroines. Help children develop a sense of belonging to "my" group without creating a negative view of other groups.

1. Understanding the biblical vision of Shalom

a. Help children to know that God creates and loves all people, that all people are one in God, and that in Christ the walls that separate us are broken down.

b. Present the Shalom vision of mutual respect, expanding the idea from exchange of favors to a more mature notion of respect as a basis of friendship and group solidarity.

c. Introduce them to people who have embraced this vision and helped to bring it more fully into the world.

d. Use the Bible story of the making of the Covenant (Abraham's story in Genesis) as preparation for making covenants with friends and with God.

e. Avoid materials that seem to give all the answers. Give children an opportunity to explore new solutions and think creatively through real problems associated with the Shalom vision.

2. Valuing all people

a. Recognize the specialness and beauty of each ethnic group and culture in our world.

b. Use materials that present ethnic and other cultural ways of life and religious beliefs in a positive rather than a belittling or deprecatory way.

c. Include ways of life other than white middle-class North Americans.

d. Expose students to heroes and heroines from many cultures using people such as Gandhi, Martin Luther King, Jr., Sojourner Truth, Dorothy Day, Cesar Chavez.

e. Avoid stereotyping minorities. Avoid the use of slang terms when speaking of ethnic groups.

f. Avoid referring to a lower standard of living in a demeaning way.

g. Do not stereotype sex roles. Present positive images of women and men doing all kinds of work.

3. Participating in creative change

a. Show Jesus' special identification with those who are poor and oppressed.

b. Use heroines and heroes who are examples of just people.

c. Emphasize the need for everyone to speak out and reaffirm the rights of each individual.

d. Include stories that show children ways of perceiving prejudice and speaking out against these ideas.

e. Include a consideration of the need to change the oppressiveness of traditional sexual relationships.

f. Give them chances to learn about the Shalom vision of justice by experiencing it as well as by talking about it.

g. Affirm rights of both students and teachers, both children and adults.

4. Using conflict creatively

a. Affirm the work of organizations that are building Shalom, such as the United Nations and Bread for the World.

b. Discuss alternatives to war.

c. Help children realize that conflict can be handled in nonviolent ways. Talk about and role-play positive ways of dealing with conflict — making fair rules, taking turns, talking things out.

d. Encourage nonviolent resolution of conflict in everyday activities.

e. Help children to evaluate use of toys of violence and the large part that television violence plays in their world.

f. Show that the Shalom vision calls for cooperation among individuals for the growth of all rather than destructive competition.

g. Play noncompetitive games.

h. Seek to help children change a win—lose situation into a win—win one.

i. Provide for shared decision-making among children and adults to teach both skill in making decisions and recognition that responsible authority means being concerned about the welfare of others.

k. Use simulation games to stimulate interest and provide experiences in solving problems in ways that create Shalom.

5. Caring for and sharing world resources

a. Help students to appreciate the beauty of the world created by God and recognize the interdependence of living things and the natural world. Make evident your own reverence for life and commitment to conserving the environment.

b. Encourage children's awareness of ways in which they can take responsibility in their world - school, family and neighborhood cleanup projects, visits to old-age homes, taking responsibility for other children.

c. Make clear that the imbalance in the possession of the world's resources is not because those living in affluent countries are smarter, wiser or better human beings. Emphasize the responsibility of those who have resources to be wise stewards and to share from their abundance. Tell stories about not over-consuming, about recycling and sharing.

d. Sensitize children to the problem of world hunger in concrete ways, as with films or making collages.

6. Choosing to live by the Shalom vision

a. Make it clear that you place a higher priority on children and their feelings and needs than you do on material things.

b. Encourage mutual appreciation of individual talents; celebrate their diversity.

c. Help children recognize that more than one correct choice is possible in solving life's problems. Encourage them to search for alternative answers and to explore the reasons for and the consequences of the decisions.

d. Include children in adult discussions of lifestyle choices and help them to see the consequences of different decisions.

e. Help children gain an understanding of the important role of citizens in the political process as part of the vision of Shalom and encourage their involvement by writing letters to officials about issues of concern.

f. Help children to recognize that they have the option of "doing something positive" in their world. Suggest ways they can be actively involved in peace concerns.

Photo: Paul Conklin

FIFTH AND SIXTH GRADERS

Children of these ages still usually think in terms of concrete realities. They need personal experience and then discussion of it more than discussion of abstract ideas. Field trips, films and games are more fruitful than only verbal discussions and debate. Stereotyping is natural at this age. A good way to counteract it and encourage the valuing of all people is through positive experiences with real people "different from us."

1. Understanding the biblical vision of Shalom
   a. Help children discover the Old and New Testament sources of the Shalom vision.
   b. Explore the notion of the Christian calling to be responsible for helping to create God's Shalom.
   c. Explore the life of Jesus to discover the different ways in which Jesus lived Shalom. "How did he treat people who felt guilty and ashamed?"

2. Valuing all people
   a. Explore the children's own stories, looking at who significant people are in their lives. "What models of peacemakers do we have?"
   b. Offer methods to help children identify and express their feelings about people of different cultures. "Where do these feelings come from? Do they help to create Shalom?"
   c. Explore materials that portray other races and their gifts and discuss the effects of racial prejudice.
   d. Affirm other cultures in the stories, illustrations, songs and audio-visuals used.
   e. Emphasize the gifts of various cultures, fostering a sense of interdependence of all people and cultures.
   f. Help children see the consequences of sex-role stereotypes and experience models of different choices about sex roles.

3. Participating in creative change
   a. Explore the nature of simple systems — water systems, drainage systems, the family. Using the family as a model, discuss the need for both interdependence *and self-determination* for individual members. Begin to build concepts of global systems.
   b. Avoid the image of developing nations as weak, backward, stupid, dependent on others.
   c. Provide help in understanding the kinds of violence that are present in our world as expressions of fears, barriers, and walls that exist between individuals and groups.
   d. Explore ways in which children can respond to these types of violence.
   e. Present heroes and heroines who have actively worked toward a Shalom vision in the world.
   f. Encourage children to visit or read about actual communities with simpler lifestyles.
   g. Nurture children's awareness of the citizen's ability to influence and affect government decisions, as in letter writing, interviews with public officials, voting.
   h. Introduce children to effective nongovernmental organizations that work toward Shalom values.

4. Using conflict creatively
   Reject violence as a way of dealing with interpersonal, intergroup and international conflict. Show the parallel between the need to talk about our interpersonal disagreements and the need for talk about our international disagreements.

5. Caring for and sharing world resources
   a. Give attention to responsible stewardship of both personal and world resources.
   b. Find ways to visualize the over-consumption in North America in comparison with developing countries. "How does this make you feel?" Explore ways of living more simply.

6. Choosing to live by the Shalom vision
   a. Emphasize the uniqueness of each individual as a valuable asset for everyone.
   b. Use activities and learning experiences that foster a sense of community in the group—mutual caring, trust, affirmation of each other.
   c. Provide help to children in realizing that having angry feelings is okay and that nonviolent means of dealing with them and managing conflict can be developed.
   d. Help children realize that they are responsible for their own actions and decisions.
   e. Help children to see the importance of values consistent with the Shalom vision, such as nonviolence in the management of conflict, respect for the uniqueness of each person, honest sharing of feelings in their homes, with their peer groups, in the community.
   f. Use news and programs on television to raise awareness of global issues; interpret these issues from the point of view of the Shalom vision.

JUNIOR HIGH YOUTH

This age is often characterized by strong feelings, by a high priority on interpersonal relationships, and by conflicting values operating in different spheres of life. Relationships with older youth and adults are important in sorting out a more integrated set of values. Resolution of conflicting values can also be helped by an atmosphere in which youth can openly discuss their feelings, problems and life situations. Because youth of this age are beginning to think abstractly, begin to introduce concepts such as economic systems, corporate responsibility and universal human rights. It is especially important for these younger youth to have older models who reflect the values of a Shalom vision.

1. *Understanding the biblical vision of Shalom*

a. Present a vision of the good society consistent with the Shalom vision. Encourage youth to take exciting risks in living out of this vision.

b. Talk about God's unconditional love for *each* of us as individuals. "No matter what I do, God never stops loving me and wanting me to live in Shalom."

c. Help youth to see the pain of the world as corporate. Pain to anyone causes pain to all and pain to God whose love is for all people.

d. Stress the "alreadiness" of Shalom as an attitude toward life that results in celebration of the goodness of life now.

e. Provide opportunities for others to share their own "faith stories."

f. Explore the meaning of words like *peace* and *justice.*

g. Develop worship programs that highlight and symbolize the Shalom vision.

2. *Valuing all people*

a. Present positive portrayals of other peoples and cultures, showing respect for and appreciation of the differences among people and the gifts of all groups.

b. Present ethnic and cultural diversity of lifestyles in stories and illustrations. Draw heroes and heroines from diverse cultures.

c. Give attention to the developing sexual identity of the youth and its relation to their cultural roles. Avoid reinforcement of the stereotypes of aggression and dominance in men, submission and passivity in women. "Both men and women can be nurses and fire fighters."

3. *Participating in creative change*

a. Help youth to see realistically the pain and suffering of all people and to look at their nation's role in inflicting that pain. Help them reject the view that their country is always right.

b. Drawing on the idea of friendship and what we need in a friendship, discuss the idea of "international friendship" and the need for people to determine their own destiny, whether they be individuals, minority groups, women or emerging nations. Introduce appropriate terms and ideas about self-development of all peoples.

c. Discuss the need to be well informed. Encourage newspaper reading and have youth share reports of news of special interest to them.

4. *Using conflict creatively*

a. Reject violence as a way of dealing with conflict and explore alternative ways of solving conflict—interpersonal through brainstorming and contracting; and conceive themselves as globally related.

b. Emphasize the reality and inevitability of frustrations and anger within and between people and the import of not smoothing it over or covering it up; help them to develop methods of dealing with these feelings constructively.

c. Help youth develop a somewhat self-regulated community of their peers by discussing and deciding on rules and standards and agreeing on how they can be maintained fairly.

5. *Caring for and sharing world resources*

a. Give attention to responsible stewardship of world and personal resources. Increase awareness of our prevalent over-consumption, including our participation in a "throwaway" mentality.

b. Deal with the complexities of political, economic and ecological realities. Among these are the tension between economic growth and the need to conserve nonrenewable resources, the conflict between regulations against industrial pollution and feared loss of jobs in the industries which pollute, the problem of safeguarding civil rights and increasing the economic opportunity of the "have-nots."

6. *Choosing to live by the Shalom vision*

a. Affirm the uniqueness of each young person and develop methods to foster each one's particular gifts for the benefit of the whole community.

b. Help youth identify and trace the sources of their values, see the effect of these values on their behavior and see how each one's personal values affect the Shalom in the community.

c. Help youth learn how to deal with authority figures. Help them to make responsible decisions in relation to particular authority figures.

d. Present the view that risk of failure is necessary if one is to develop one's full potential and that often risk is possible only when we feel support from a community.

e. Design activities that incorporate planning and service on the part of the youth, in accord with the Shalom vision—raising money for the hungry or visiting shut-ins.

f. Present the view that we can influence the structures in which we live. Help youth to see patriotism as obedience, but also as participation in making decisions for the society in the light of the Shalom vision.

g. Look at how one person can expand personal effectiveness by joining a group that represents Shalom values.

SENIOR HIGH YOUTH

Interpersonal relationships are still very important at this age. Therefore, opportunities for discussion and sharing among themselves and with adults who embody the Shalom vision are essential. Now is the time to help youth critically examine the existing institutional structures around them in relation to their own developing sense of justice. Simulation games and exposure to real organizations concretely involved in the solution of social problems are useful.

1. Understanding the biblical vision of Shalom

a. Look at the different ways the People of God have organized their social-political life—theocracy, federation, small primary groups of friends living in community. "What values are common to them all?"

b. Read and discuss biographies of people who have lived a life of Shalom.

c. Explore the idea of occupational accountability and discuss vocational choices in terms of our "Christian calling."

d. Discuss the equal importance that all nations and peoples have to God. The Covenant relationship was not a special privilege but a special responsibility to help all nations to know God's love.

2. Valuing all people

a. Use the awareness of world events youth have to reinforce a sense of global consciousness in terms of what it would mean to allow all people to develop wholeness of life, health and joy.

b. Help youth affirm the value of social diversity, become aware of others kinds of people as valuable and conceive themselves as globally related.

c. Discuss the arbitrariness of our preferences and customs and their origin in our particular social learning.

3. Participating in creative change

a. Encourage the development of the sense of justice as freedom for all to be self-determining.

b. Present the concept of world resources as belonging to all people.

c. Help youth to become sensitive to racist and sexist language.

d. Plan activities to expose youth to a variety of organizations inside and outside the church that reflect the Shalom vision and values. Included might be well-supervised participation with adults in demonstrations and protests.

e. Focus on concrete cases in which the church as an organization is taking a role in working toward solutions to social problems—the boycott against promotion of baby formula in developing countries or World Peace Tax Fund advocacy in the U.S. Congress.

4. Using conflict creatively

a. Deal with life situations in which youth have problems of identity and feel different or alone—at school, home, church, in working relationships. Help students to discover the Gospel in these situations.

b. Help youth develop nonmilitant, nondestructive methods of resolving conflict.

c. Distinguish the "ability to be violent" from "being powerful."

d. Through role-play and discussion, help youth to understand how to use active listening in situations of disagreement.

5. Caring for and sharing world resources

a. Emphasize a sense of stewardship regarding creation's natural resources.

b. Explore the causes of hunger and poverty and what can be done about them, especially by the relevant non-governmental organizations.

6. Choosing to live by the Shalom vision

Help youth to…

a. See peacefulness as an active and creative process.

b. Develop a sense of pride in geopolitical, racial and sexual identity, but one that does not belittle others.

c. Explore the implications of Shalom for issues such as sexuality, sex roles and life styles.

d. Give many chances to experience as well as talk about the concepts being expressed.

DISARMAMENT CAMPAIGNS IN CANADA

The following materials are used by permission of Disarmament Campaigns, The Hague, Netherlands

Some people are willing to initiate action even when they must act alone or with only a few others. More people will consider taking action when they know of the experiences of others.

The stories in this section are offered as a sampler of the kinds of action which people with a vision for peace have been able to take. They are illustrative of similar activity happening in many places around the world.

An international newsletter reporting such actions against the arms race is called DISAMAMENT CAMPAIGNS. Reports are made in each issue of activity around the world. The reports given here are from that periodical.

To show the worldwide nature of peace action, note the items in the May 1982 issue. Among them are stories from Canada on local nuclear free zones, the dangers of the nuclear chain and information on uranium mining. Also included are notes from the section called "Around the World."

To bring visions to reality requires action. Such action is more noticeable and like to bring results if it is done by large groups of people. If enough people begin to move together with a shared vision of peace, our government may be willing to begin to act differently than it does now.

LOCAL NUCLEAR FREE ZONES

(Reported in May 1982)

By Dwight Burkhardt

In September 1981, Project Ploughshares initiated a campaign to declare Canada a Nuclear Weapon Free Zone (NWFZ). Its three year commitment to wage the campaign was taken in response to the urging by the United Nations for the creation of such zones. The commitment was also a sign of support of European efforts to establish nuclear free zones and the U.S. freeze campaign. The NWFZ proposal is seen as a means to further the aims of the project to seek alternative strategies for security in Canadia that do not rely upon the threat of force or nuclear genocide.

To date the campaign has introduced the idea of the NWFZ into the Canadian disarmament public debate. Project Ploughshares has carried out initial research into the specifics of a NWFZ and the implications for Canadian defense policies and military operations. It is expected that research will continue into specific policy changes and operational procedures of the Canadian government and its armed forces as the campaign continues. Support for the proposal is being sought through the dissemination of information and action suggestions to small groups, churches and other organizations across Canada. New educational materials, audio-visuals, public lectures and media interviews are being prepared and presented. In addition, signatures and endorsements of a petition calling for the declaration of a Canadian Nuclear Weapon Free Zone are being solicited.

As the campaign continues, members of Project Ploughshares hope that other organizations will adopt the NWFZ proposal and incorporate its objectives into their ongoing efforts. The project is presently devising a strategy for church involvement in the campaign. Many churches are already actively involved in supporting the proposal through resolutions of their governing bodies and distribution of campaign materials to local churches. A significant development has been the release of a position paper of 78 prominent Canadians calling for a new direction in Canadian foreign and defense policy, including the declaration of a NWFZ in Canada. Contact: Project Ploughshares, Conrad Grebel College, Waterloo, Ontario N2L, Canada.

THE NUCLEAR CHAIN (reported in July/August 1982)

By Barbara Fields, Ayn Lowry, Ann Kirschermann

In 1979, the accident at Three Mile Island focused the world's attention on the dangers of nuclear power. Two years later in the fall of 1981, one million people marched through the streets of Europe to protest the deployment of U.S. nuclear weapons. Is there a connection between these two issues? If so, what are they? Can we march to the United Nations and demand disarmament and a nuclear weapons freeze and at the same time allow "peaceful" nuclear development to continue?

While most antinuclear activities acknowledge similarities between nuclear weapons and nuclear power, two separate movements have sprung up to challenge two different uses of atomic energy. And now that the nuclear disarmament movement has gained worldwide attention, the nuclear power issue has taken a back seat. The two remain separate and distinguishable issues of public policy. Or so nuclear proponents would have us believe.

Distinction between civilian and military use of atomic energy is largely superficial. Both share the same technology and historical development. Both pose similar threats of radiation exposure and environmental contamination. In the words of Michio Kaku, physicist and professor at City College of New York, "Nuclear power and nuclear weapons are two sides of the same coin. They are controlled by the same people, produced by the same corporations and serve the same political and financial interests. They give off the same radioactive poisons, generate the same deadly waste that nobody yet knows what to do with...and both threaten catastrophic destruction. The people who brought us Hiroshima also bring us Harrisburg."

Nuclear power plants and nuclear bombs are fueled by

the same basic raw material—uranium. The major corporations involved in the uranium industry are often the same corporations that play a major role in the production of nuclear weapons. In the early stages of the nuclear chain—mining and milling—there is no distinction in how the uranium will ultimately be used. Both steps present dangers in their own right.

Huge amounts of radioactivity are released. Milling and mining not only create severe environmental and health problems for miners and surrounding communities, but together constitute a far greater waste problem, in terms of volume, than either nuclear power plant operation or nuclear weapons production.

Following mining and milling, the next major step is enrichment in which the part of the uranium used to make a chain reaction is separated. Once separated, this uranium can be used in nuclear reactors or can be used to make Hiroshima-type uranium bombs. Separation technology was devised by people working on the development of atomic bombs during World War II.

It is impossible to generate electricity in an uranium-based reactor without at the same time producing plutonium. Consequently, every nuclear power plant produces on the average between 300 and 500 pounds of plutonium each year—enough for approximately 25 to 40 Nagasaki-type bombs. Thus any country with nuclear power plants automatically has the potential for nuclear weapons. Countries such as India, Pakistan, Israel and South Africa—who ardently claim to pursue "peaceful" nuclear development—have simultaneously been able to develop their nuclear weapons capability, thus following in the footsteps of the five major nuclear weapon states.

One method of obtaining nuclear weapons materials from nuclear power plants is to reprocess this fuel after it has been irradiated. This procedure, preprocessing, separates out unfissioned uranium and plutonium from the spent reactor fuel rods, both of which can then be enriched to weapons grade. And to deliver these nuclear payloads, technology has steadily progressed since Hiroshima to develop more refined, versatile and accurate weapons. These weapons have served to increase military dependence on nuclear weapons, thus integrating nuclear weapons into war fighting strategies and making the "unthinkable" more possible. Dimensions of the nuclear chain that are present in other countries include enrichment in The Netherlands, power plants in the Philippines, fast breeder reactors and preprocessing in France, plutonium production and weapons research in the United States, weapons testing in Moruroa, weapons deployment in Italy and waste in Japan and the Pacific. Both weapons and power production have generated vast amounts of nuclear waste which pose a threat to the environments for thousands of years and which no one knows how to dispose of safely. Nuclear technology in any form poses environmental, social and economic costs that make it unacceptable. Nuclear power plants give off radioactive pollution. Nuclear weapons production plants give off even greater amounts of radioactvity. The weapons themselves are tools of mass murder. A choice for nuclear power is a choice for nuclear weapons. Thus people caught in every link in the nuclear chain are directly affected by these decisions. And so is everyone else.

MINING: CANADA

The antinuclear movement in Saskatchewan, Canada, is confronted with a uranium mining industry that is thriving under some of the best conditions in the world. Uranium in Saskatchewan is unusually rich and near the surface, meaning mining costs are relatively low.

For example, officials of one company brag that they were able to mine nine million dollars worth of uranium in one day. In addition, a stable investment climate is offered by the provincial and federal governments through direct partnerships and numerous subsidies. The uranium is located in the far north of the province in a sparsely populated area which miners say is inhabited "only by Indians." These conditions have insulated the uranium mining industry from certain difficulties experienced in other parts of the world.

Presently about five million kilograms of yellowcake (the final precipitate formed in the milling of uranium ore) are being produced in Saskatchewan each year. This amount was expected to double by 1983. In terms of the production of solid and liquid toxic wastes, Saskatchewan government reports indicate about 2.5 million kilograms are produced per year. These wastes have rendered many water bodies immediately downstream from the mines unsuitable for drinking and have contaminated aquatic life. There is no known method of stopping the contamination.

Since the mid-1970s, resistance by the antinuclear movement has primarily taken the form of participation in government inquiries and publication of literature. A small victory was won in 1979 when resistance forced the cancellation of a uranium refinery planned for the central, populated area of the province.

Although the uranium mining boom continues in Saskatchewan, a number of factors have contributed to making the future of the industry more insecure. Some of the major reasons are the collapse of uranium price on the world market, economic disintegration of the commercial reactor industry and the growing realization of the connection between uranium and nuclear weapons.

The antinuclear movement in Saskatchewan has mushroomed to include environmental coalitions, church groups, native people, phsyicians, lawyers and many others. Despite a relatively broad base and high level of awareness, resistance to uranium mining and nuclear proliferation is at present unorganized. Public information meetings hosted by local resistance groups are occurring regularly.

The most common topic is the connection between Saskatchewan uranium and nuclear weapons. Also, a direct action campaign to stop the transportation of uranium has recently begun. The focus is where it is going to. So far the "stop uranium transport" campaign has taken the form of phone calls and letters to the major transportation company involved, as well as peaceful protests at company offices.

Plans to continue pressure include more public meetings, and peaceful truck blockades beginning this summer (1982). Contact: Uranium Traffic Network, Box 7192, Saskatoon Saskatchewan, Canada S7K 4J2

FALKLAND FALLOUT

The struggle between Argentina and Great Britain over the Falkland Islands has raised concerns, once again, about Argentina's nuclear program, specifically its capacity to manufacture a nuclear bomb. While defending Britain's military actions against Argentina, the Canadian government has also stated it plans to go ahead with the shipment of $4 million worth of nuclear equipment to Argentina.

Under a contract signed between Canada and Argentina in 1977, Canada agreed to deliver the equipment before the end of June 1982. Despite reports that Argentina is close to having a bomb, External Affairs Minister Mark MacGuigan commented on the technology transfer, "We have an agreement with the Argentinians in which they will not use our nuclear technology for any nonpeaceful purpose, and we have no reason at all to think they will depart from that."

Using the dangerous logic once applied towards U.S. nuclear sales to India, MacGuigan claims that Argentina would have to break its contract with Canada if it were to build a bomb. Having a contract supposedly gives Canada some leverage over the Argentinian program, yet all indications are that Argentina is proceeding with bomb production.

The next crisis involving Argentina could well be a nuclear one.

CRUISE PROTEST

On April 8, [1982], in a third act of civil disobedience in less than a year, the Cruise Missile Conversion Project, World Emergency Peterborough and a number of other disarmament groups blocked the entrance to the day shift at Litton Systems Canada (a contractor for Cruise components) in suburban Toronto.

We were in place at 7 a.m. and prevented traffic from entering until 11:30 a.m. The blockaders went in waves.

After two groups had been arrested and hauled away, a third group of a dozen people poured their blood in an unbroken line across the driveway. By this time workers had either walked in or had gone home.

At 11 a.m., 15 more were arrested and shortly thereafter another group of 6 were arrested. In all, 34 people were arrested, charged with trespassing and given summonses to appear in provincial court on May 10. We are beginning some joint projects with United Auto Workers...sponsoring joint educational events mainly centered around the Lucas Aerospace Shop Stewards Committee. We are meeting further with education department people, staff representatives, union organizers and local members.

The issue of Canada allowing testing of the Cruise missile in northern Alberta has become a focus of nationwide protest. There is talk of our direction campaign moving to Ottawa. Contact: Cruise Missile Conversion Project, 730 Bathurst St., Toronto, Ontario M53 2R4, Canada.

CANADIAN PEACE CARAVAN (reported in December 1982)

By Jeanne Shaw

The Canadian Peace Caravan is planning to travel through areas of British Columbia (B.C.), Alberta, and Saskatchewan during October and November 1982 raising awareness about the Cruise Missile specifically, and militarism in general. The final destination of the Caravan will be Cold Lake, Alberta, where a peace camp is to be set up and a house has been donated for this purpose.

The objectives of the Peace Caravan are:

1. to travel through B.C., Alberta, and Saskatchewan, especially the smaller, more remote communities to help form a network of groups working for disarmament and peace;

2. to meet with students, native people, church groups and others to facilitate their learning about and organizing around the issue of disarmament and peace;

3. to share our organizing, group process and communication skills with the groups we meet;

4. to work with groups and individuals to find non-violent strategies to respond to growing militarism and to the testing and construction of the Cruise Missile.

Peace Caravan plans to stay at the Cold Lake Peace Camp at least through the winter. Our objectives in being at the camp include:

1. being part of a peaceful presence in a military area;

2. helping the Camp become a western centre for information on the Cruise while staying in close contact with those in the east;

3. meeting civilian, military and native people on a one-to-one basis and helping each of us gain a better understanding of the other;

4. gathering and disseminating information about the history of the area, specifically as to the relationship between the military base and the native people (the base was established in the middle of a reserve);

5. helping work towards Cold Lake becoming a center for non-violent action and training;

6. resisting the testing of the Cruise Missile in Canada.

We will be sending out information of our ongoing experiences to the media and to groups and individuals. We hope to make a slide-tape show of our experiences as well. We are asking groups and individuals who feel that this is a worthwhile project to help us with the financial costs. Contact: Cold Lake Peace Camp Committee, 5, 1134-5th Avenue NW, Calgary, Alberta, Canada.

SCHWERTER ZU PFLUGSCHAREN

Swords into Plowshares: Christian Witness by Youth in
the German Democratic Republic

by Walter Schenck

*Often in history, it has been the young people who have
moved to bring the hope for a better future into reality.
This has been true with those committed both to war and
to peace. Certainly it is the young who are expected to fight
in wars.*

*One group of North American youth is Young
Christians for Global Justice (YCGJ). One of the adults
who has work with YCGJ as a staff advisor is Walter
Schenck. He and two young people, one from the United
States and one from Canada, were invited to participate
in the Third European Ecumenical Youth Conference
which explored issues of faith and justice. Held in the
spring of 1982, the conference took place in a village in the
German Democratic Republic (GDR/East Germany).*

*This article is his report of his experience of that
meeting. He describes the place of the church, and peace
ministry in which its young people are involved. It is
included here to illustrate the commitment which
Christian in both the "East" and the "West" have made for
peace and the action they have taken to let those in power
know of their convictions.*

*Schenck is with the General Board of Global Ministries
of the United Methodist Church. His responsibilities
include working with young adults on global issues.*

Surprised by their government's defensive response,
young Christians in the German Democratic Republic
(GDR—East Germany) have found that wearing a patch
on their arms caused a major debate between their
church and their government.

The government of the GDR has banned the wearing of
a cloth badge popular among many youth. It depicts a
metal-worker forging a sword into a plow, encircled with
the biblical quotation, "Schwerter zu Pflugscharen —
Micha IV" (Swords into Plowshares—Micah 4).

The symbol is a representation of the statue given to
the United Nations in New York City by the Soviet
Union. The government feared that the patch was being
"misused" to "express a way of thinking hostile to the
government and to participate in an illegal political
movement."

Much of the turmoil was fueled on February 13, 1982,
when over 4,000 youth gathered in Dresden to commemo-
rate the bombing of that city in World War II. In 1945,
British and American fliers fire-bombed the city, ruining
it and killing some 35,000 people. During this annual
commemoration a peace forum was held at one of the
historic churches nearly destroyed during the bombing
raids of 37 years before.

In the months preceding this memorial event, the small
three-inch patch portraying the biblical imperative to
make peace was circulated among church youth. It had
been developed and distributed by the churches in
November 1981 for use in the annual "Decade for
Peace"—a 10-day emphasis on peace in which youth study

the international implications of the relationship
between faith and justice.

Not believing their actions to be contrary to the
government's position, these youth were taken aback by
the strong, critical reaction which East Berlin officials
made to their witness for peace. Asserting that the GDR
was already participating in the movement for peace
through the Warsaw Pact, the government saw no need
to have another, independent (and unsanctioned) effort
develop.

They were especially concerned that a peace movement
sponsored by the churches might take a political stance
against the government. Such a development, the government feared, could lead to a broad-based conflict in
other arenas. A precedent, which would be a departure
from the basically amicable church-state relationships
which have developed over the past decade. The GDR is
a small country. A large proportion of its population,
about 70 percent, are active church members and it has
a common border with troubled Poland. Both facts make
church-state relationships a primary concern of the
government.

It was within this rather dramatic context that representatives of various national organizations of young
Christians in Europe gathered in an old, medieval castle
nestled in the south central hills of the GDR. Here in the
village of Burgscheidungen, members of the Ecumenical
Youth Council of Europe (EYCE) convened the Third
European Ecumenical Youth Conference under the
theme, *"Glaube and Gerechtigkeit"* (Faith and Justice).

For seven days delegations from nearly every Eastern
and Western European nation came together to study
and to celebrate Easter. In addition, guests were present
representing other global regions including Asia, the
Pacific, Africa, the Middle East, North and South

America. North America was represented by a delegation from EYCE's colleague organization, Young Christians for Global Justice (YCGJ). Those there included Michael Thompson of the Anglican Church of Canada, then Canadian co-chair of YCGJ, and Andres Thomas of the United Methodist Church, a U.S. member of the Steering Committee, and this writer.

With the ground-swell of antinuclear, pro-disarmament sentiment significantly altering both U.S. and GDR politics, defense-minded administrations were caught off-guard. Given this reality, the North American visitors felt more than a small measure of empathetic solidarity with their Christian sisters and brothers in the GDR.

Fresh in the North Americans' memories were reactionary statements from their governments' highest officials who mouthed agreement to popular demands for a nuclear freeze, but wanted the freeze only after achieving an ill-defined and illusive superiority to the Soviet Union's arsenal. It was the same, even familiar double-speak language that Heinz Hoffman, the GDR's Secretary of Defense used in a March 25, 1982, statement before the GDR Parliament. In this statement he asserted that the road was a very long one which will lead to "one day (when) we should very much like to scrap our weapons, but at the present time socialism needs both our plowshares and our swords."

In April, governmental actions were being taken to enforce the new policy as some GDR youth delegates to the EYCE Conference were delayed on the way to the meeting. Caught wearing the badge on the sleeves of their jackets, they were stopped by transit police, then detained by local police.

One youth who was held for five hours was finally required to remove the badge from his coat. As with others who had similarly been caught, he cut out its center leaving an empty white circle and a new badge of real protest. Some concerned mothers had sewn a small patch of black cloth over the badge. Still others simply continued to wear the patch, either on their outer clothing, or, less conspicuously, on wallets carried in their pockets.

On Easter evening, immediately following a rain and hail storm, participants gathered together with the local people in the nearby city of Erfurt for an ecumenical worship service. Crowded into the chilly, unheated sanctuary of the Predigekirche, they warmed its cavernous nave where Martin Luther had preached with songs of "Adoramus Te Domine" and "Christ Ist Erstanden(Christ Is Risen)" and "Herr, gib uns deinige Frieden (God, Give Us Your Peace)." Even our damp clothing and wet shoes resting on the cold stone floor lost their discomfort in the quiet joy of the celebration.

It was Werner Krusche, bishop of Erfurt who preached that evening, addressing directly the issue on each of our minds, especially those of young GDR Christians. These young people listened attentively, some moving to the edges of their seats as they heard their Bishop declare to this international congregation in English, French and German so everyone could understand:

"The history of the missionary church started with an insignificant group of frightened men...(who) came together behind locked doors. It is a sign of fear when doors are locked, when entrances are walled up, communications impeded and borders sealed. Fear of the infiltration of ideas...fear of experiencing reality which is not in harmony with our own artificial image of reality;

fear of opinions we are not permitted to have publicly.

"In the domain of fear even the peace symbol of peaceful young Christians becomes a dangerous object which must be confiscated."

In the midst of this highly charged occasion, this writer experienced one of those rare moments when, if only for an instant, the reality of Christian community was understood with clarity. The "principalities and powers" which transcend national and ideological boundaries became visible, while the Spirit which binds faithful Christians embraced us tightly. In those moments I understood anew the common mission to which the global Christian community is called.

In the faces of these earnest Christians was not an urge to tear down either their government or anyone else's government. Rather there was a strong desire to move us all toward peace *and* justice. This is not to say that they were not sharply critical, even fearful of the USA-NATO nuclear forces stationed only a few miles from their homes—especially the horrid neutron bomb. They were. But the reality of being caught geographically in the middle had brought them to a renewed understanding of Christian faith.

The church occupies a special place in the social fabric of the GDR. It is granted a position of relative independence not accorded to any other institution. Within this old society's relatively new social system, only organizations officially sanctioned by the government are permitted.

The church in this situation is, as one pastor characterized it, "a free space." Freedom of expression within the religious community is both encouraged and honored even though the church is often observed by state agents. Its leaders realize that this special standing in the community has provided for the church both an added responsibility and a special opportunity, especially in its ministry with youth and young adults.

Encouraged by its openness, large numbers of young Christians have recently reentered the church's life often accompanied by their friends without a religious background. Even relatively small churches have a high proportion of youth. As one of the "free" or "confessing" churches in the GDR, the United Methodist Church (UMC) is considerably smaller than the larger *Evangelische Kirchen and Evangelische Landeskirchen,* the current expression of the Reformed Church and former Lutheran national church in Germany.

Although the local UMC in Erfurt may only have 100 members, 50 children and 20 youth are also active in its program. Participation of young Christians in the Reformed and Lutheran churches is proportionately greater. Along with personal problems and biblical studies, concern for Third World people and world peace focuses their discussion and action.

Across the GDR these churches have responded with strong support for youth, especially for those wearing the controversial sign of peace. The executive committees of the eight regional Reformed and Lutheran Churches and Council of (free) Churches issued a joint statement in March 1982. The statement supported the youth saying that it is "our Christian hope that someday God will create a world in which we human beings do not need weapons to protect us." In addition, many synods made separate declarations on the issue.

The Gorlitz Synod of the Evangelical Church voted unanimously to stand with the young people, deploring the "attacks, slanderous statements and painful accusations" to which they had been subjected. The Evangelical Church of Saxony in its statement, also voting unanimously, declared that not only was the government's position on the peace patch a serious mistake, but that the government's ban "destroys the trust of the young people."

Many GDR youth have also been pressing for a civilian alternative to the required military service, a cause that has been taken up and promoted by the churches. Although current policy permits anyone by simple declaration to enter the noncombatant *bausoldaten* (construction corps), it remains an option only within the military. Many would prefer to serve their country in civilian social service positions such as hospital aides, social workers, and through other community service agencies. But pressures arising from a low birthrate in recent years have resulted in a strain to fill national quotas for military service, including the training of career officers, as required by the Warsaw Pact.

This situation has made consideration of non-military national service a difficult matter. This is especially so, GDR citizens say, with the threat of the NATO neutron bomb looming over Europe. During the winter of January 1983 visitors returning from the GDR reported that though the peace patch is still outlawed, the *Schwerter Zu Pflugscharen* symbol was used during the annual "Decade for Peace" program of the church in November 1982. It was reproduced with a government-issued printing permit on bookmarks for that occasion.

Earlier, however, the GDR government had issued its own government-approved "peace" badge. A rectangular patch in the familiar style of an international pictograph, it shows a bomb sitting on its end sporting the American flag. Superimposed over it is the negative, diagonal red stripe. Across the top printed in capital letters are the words, "GEGEN NATO" (Oppose NATO).

But the irony is that it is precisely the threat of nuclear holocaust which has precipitated the wide-spread movements for peace, justice and disarmament not only in Europe, but around the world. And it appears to be a central factor in the GDR as well. There is a very familiar ring which one hears in the official rhetoric defending the arms buildup in both the East and the West.

Hearing about the "long road to peace..." in the GDR is very much like hearing President Ronald Reagan say on the occasion of the June 12, 1982, Peace March in New York City, "I would be at the head of the march if I thought it would do any good." Certainly more than anything else such defensive statements have raised up the common notes now echoing throughout what can now be understood only as a global movement for peace and justice.

Perhaps it will be as Bishop Krusche put it in the conclusion of his Easter sermon:

"Dear friends, we are Easter pilgrims, envoys of the risen Christ; we here in the GDR and you in the countries to which you will soon be returning. Surrounded and attended by God's peace, we have received the gift of life through the new creation, authorized to liberate those who have fallen into sin. Where the followers of the risen Christ are to be found things will not remain unchanged. Jesus Christ's New Age of Peace will make itself felt. There, each day is a new awakening and there is life really worthwhile."

Adapted from an article in New World Outlook November 1982. Edited for this publication.

THE COURAGE TO CARE

(Can be sung to the tune: "Theme from Chariots of Fire")

This world in transition, old forms torn apart
Creates a new mission, demands a new heart.
The new world is crushing the one that we knew.
Our minds barely touching the change rushing
   through.

   But ours is a dream that gives the world
     A vision to share
   And ours is the hope that gives the people
     Courage to care.

The glove is a village four billion strong.
We're building the home where each one can belong.
The cry is beyond us, it beckons us on.
Our passion upon us, eternity-long.

   Chorus

If ever a singer were needed to sing,
If ever a dreamer were needed to dream,
If ever a people were called on to stand,
It's surely this moment, it's surely this land.*

   Hold on to the dream that gives the world
     A vision to share
   And cherish the hope that gives the people
     Courage to care.

   Repeat the chorus.

*Land means the whole earth, not any one nation.

*Song used by permission of the Institute of Cultural affairs,
4750 North Sheridan Road, Chicago, Illinois, 60640.*

ADVICE TO A DRAFTEE

by Leo Tolstoy

The Hessian army of 1899 was a peacetime army. The penalty for evading conscription though was death. A young man by the name of Ernst Schramm facing conscription had apparently written to Count Leo Tolstoy expressing his concern about participating in the army. Their exchange of letters is lost except for this one which seems to be the end of their correspondence. From the content of this letter, Tolstoy is responding to questions which Schramm had still been raising.

This letter was addressed to Schramm in Darmstadt. The post office forwarded it to Aschaffenburg in Bavaria, leaving us to infer that Schramm decided not to be drafted, but to change countries instead.

The advice from Tolstoy has an amazingly current ring to it, given the required registration of young men in the United States. Thousands are refusing to register. As this is written in June 1983, the staff of just one small denomination's peace and justice office knows of more than 50 who have not registered. They assume that there are many more. Young men, like Enten Eller, the first of these young men to be tried and convicted, sound much like Martin Luther saying, "Here I stand. I can do no other. God calls me to this position."

In my last letter I answered your question as well as I could. It is not only Christians but all just people who must refuse to become soldiers—that is, to be ready on another's command (for this what a soldier's duty actually consists of) to kill all those one is ordered to kill. The question as you state it—which is more useful, to become a good teacher or to suffer for rejecting conscription?—is falsely stated. The question is falsely stated because it is wrong for us to determine our actions according to their results, to view actions merely as useful or destructive. In the choice of our actions we can be led by their advantages or disadvantages only when the action themselves are not opposed to the demands of morality.

We can stay home, go abroad or concern ourselves with farming or science according to what we find useful for ourselves or others; for neither in domestic life, foreign travel, farming nor science is there anything immoral. But under no circumstance can we inflict violence on people, torture or kill them because we think such acts could be of use to us or to others. We cannot and may not do such things, especially because we can never be sure of the results of our actions. Often actions which seem the most advantageous of all turn out in fact to be destructive; and the reverse is also true.

The question should not be stated: which is more useful, to be a good teacher or to go to jail for refusing conscription? but rather: what should a man do who has been called upon for military service—that is, called upon to kill or to prepare himself to kill?

And to this question, for a person who understands the true meaning of military service and who wants to be moral, there is only one clear and incontrovertible answer: such a person must refuse to take part in military service no matter what consequences this refusal may have. It may seem to us that this refusal could be futile or even harmful, and that it would be a far more useful thing, after serving one's time, to become a good village teacher. But in the same way, Christ could have judged it more useful for himself to be a good carpenter and submit to all the principles of the Pharisees than to die in obscurity as he did, repudiated and forgotten by everyone.

Moral acts are distinguished from all other acts by the fact that they operate independently of any predictable advantage to ourselves or to others. No matter how dangerous the situation may be of a man who finds himself in the power of robbers who demand that he take part in plundering, murder and rape, a moral person cannot take part. Is not military service the same thing? Is one not required to agree to the deaths of all those one is commanded to kill?

But how can one refuse to do what everyone does, what everyone finds unavoidable and necessary? Or must one do what no one does and what everyone considers unnecessary or even stupid and bad? No matter how strange it sounds, this strange argument is the main one offered against those moral acts which in our times face you and every other person called up for military service. But this argument is even more incorrect than the one which would make a moral action dependent upon considerations of advantage.

If I, in finding myself in a crowd of running people, run with the crowd without knowing where, it is obvious that I have given myself up to mass hysteria; but if by chance I should push my way to the front, or be gifted with sharper sight than the others or receive information that this crowd was racing to attack human beings and toward its own corruption, would I really not stop and tell the people what might rescue them? Would I go on running and do these things which I knew to be bad and corrupt? This is the situation of every individual called up for military service, if he knows what military service means.

I can well understand that you, a young man full of life, loving and loved by your mother, friends, perhaps a young woman, think with a natural terror about what awaits you if you refuse conscription; and perhaps you will not feel strong enough to bear the consequences of refusal, and knowing your weakness, will submit and become a soldier. I understand completely, and I do not for a moment allow myself to blame you, knowing very well that in your place I might perhaps do the same thing.

Only do not say that you did it because it was useful or because everyone does it. If you did it, know that you did wrong. In every person's life there are moments in which he can know himself, tell himself who he is, whether he is a man who values his human dignity above his life or a weak creature who does know his dignity and is concerned merely with being useful (chiefly to himself). This is the situation of a man who goes out to defend his honor in a duel or a soldier who goes into battle (although here the concepts of life are wrong).

It is the situation of a doctor or a priest called to someone sick with plague, or a man in a burning house or a sinking ship who must decide whether to let the weaker go first or shove them aside and save himself. It is the situation of a man in poverty who accepts or rejects a bribe. And in our times, it is the situation of a man called to military service. For a man who knows its significance, the call to he army is perhaps the only opportunity for him to behave as a morally free creature and fulfill the highest requirement of his life—or else merely to keep his advantage in sight like an animal and thus remain slavishly submissive and servile until humanity becomes degraded and stupid.

For these reasons I answered your questions whether one has to refuse to do military service with a categorical "yes"—if you understand the meaning of military service (and if you did not understand it then, you do now) and if you want to behave as a moral person living in our times must.

Please excuse me if these words are harsh. The subject is so important that one cannot be careful enough in expressing oneself so as to avoid false interpretation.

April 7, 1899   Leo Tolstoy

Translated by Rodney G. Dennis. Reprinted by permission of the Harvard College Library. Copyright by the Houghton Library.

Photo: Walt Kleine

CORN FOR FOOD, NOT MONEY FOR WEAPONS—A FORM OF TAX PROTEST

by Chris Schroeder

After 30 years of refusing to pay part of his taxes, Ralph Dull, an Ohio farmer, decided that a more dramatic way of making his witness was needed. This chapter was written by Chris Schroeder for the newsletter of the Church of the Brethren District Office of Southern Ohio.

Some Christians have a conviction that they must protest the payment of that portion of taxes used for the preparation of war, a destructive and, in their minds, sinful purpose. The extent of witness and protest varies widely. One man and his wife have never paid taxes because they have never allowed their incomes to reach taxable levels. they and their several children have lived through the year raising chickens, goats and vegetables in order to live without money.

Other people give money to the United Nations or other organizations in the amount of the calculated tax. By notifying the government of their action, they risk having the tax plus interest taken from them and it usually is. But their action is protest.

This story is included not as a suggestion of how all readers should or could respond to taxation for building weapons, but as a stimulus to thinking and acting in some way to bring visions of peace into reality.

Ralph Dull, 53, of Brookville, Ohio, is a man of principle. Each year since 1950 he has refused to pay a portion of his income taxes.

In 1982, he chose a new way to bring the issue to the minds of the public. On April 15, he parked his loaded 2-ton grain truck in front of the Federal Building in downtown Dayton. He had come to offer the Internal Revenue Service 325 bushels of corn in lieu of taxes he owed on his 1981 income.

Dull stated that the action was "to dramatize and emphasize the need for the Federal government to turn its priorities around and support constructive people programs rather than use our resources for an arms race that is murderous and suicidal. The government should balance the budget by reducing military spending by at least $100 billion."

Signs on the sides and back of the big red truck read: "Food for People—Yes! Taxes for Arms Race—No!" "Taxes for Peace—World Peace Tax Fund."

As Ralph Dull stepped out of the cab of his truck, he was faced with several microphones. He answered the questions of the people from the media. One reporter asked, "Will this action change anyone's mind?"

Dull answered, "I have no way of knowing, but I feel that many persons are examining their old positions and we want to offer encouragement for them to put, for instance, the arms race at a very low priority."

Then Dull walked into the building where he had what he called a friendly, 20-minute meeting with a representative of the IRS. He asked the IRS to sign a statement acknowledging the value of the grain as well as guaranteeing that its value would be used only for non-military purposes.

The IRS representative, a former farmer, refused to sign the statement but admitted that he sympathized somewhat with Dull's conviction. "But I am just doing my job," he said.

Ralph remarked with a slight smile that if no one would collect the taxes, there would be no arms race. Later he stated, "If the World Peace Tax Fund bill were passed, the IRS director could sign the statement that I presented to him, asking for a guarantee that the value of the corn in payment for taxes would not be used for military purposes."

Dull then took the corn to a local purchasing agent and sold it for $777. The check was made out to Church World Service. It was given to the National Farmers Organization for their Food for Poland project.

Ralph urges that grain and not military equipment be shipped around the world by the U.S. government. The "corn for tax payment" idea was Ralph's. The project was a cooperative one, involving his family.

Daughter-in-law Sue made the signs for the truck. Son Mike and daughter Becky saved parking spots for the truck in front of the Federal Building. Son Kevin helped load the corn.

People of the Brethren Peacemakers of Southern Ohio and others passed out explanations of the action. Petitions were available to be signed calling on the state legislature to ask for a immediate freeze on nuclear weapons by both the United States and the Soviet Union.

There was only one angry man who wanted to argue. He thought it important that we hold the Soviets in fear of us. Ralph's response was, "We often use the word 'deterrent.' How can scaring the living daylights out of another people eventually lead to people living cooperatively on the face of the earth? The Russian threat to us is tame compared to what we are doing to ourselves. We have met the enemy and he is us. Our attitude toward Russia as a nation and as a people must change. We must learn to rejoice with them when there is real improvement and weep with them when there is real misfortune. We are to love people no matter where they are, and to love someone is to wish them well."

Soft-spoken, but articulate, Ralph says, "I've been asked how I respond to the charge that my action is naive and silly and impractical. The nonviolent, reconciliatory, constructive approach is the practical way. It is rational and has a future. What is impractical about friendship?"

Dull further states, "The ancestors of Brethren, Quakers and Mennonites came to this country from Europe seeking religious freedom and freedom from conscription and participation in war. It is a human rights issue that forces conscientious objectors to pay for death and destruction. Apart from the religious aspect of this issue, what this symbolic action lifts up for consideration is 'human decency'. It is vulgar to squander material and human resources while there is so much opportunity to relieve existing human misery."

Used by Permission of the Southern Ohio Herald. Edited for this publication

THE ANDREE WAGNER STORY *by Sam Blackwell*

Hundreds of peace groups exist throughout the world. It is impossible to keep track. In a spring 1982 issue of a Boston newspaper, over 80 organizations were listed and only a few of the church-related ones were included in the list. Professional people, those in unions, people of various ages, those with slightly different causes have drawn together around peace-related issues. The range of possibilities of response are represented in the many groups. Regardless of individual approaches or perspectives, persons are lightly to find a group of other individuals with similar views who at taking action.

The report of Jobs with Peace is included here as an example of one of those many groups. It was chosen because it is one which has been able to enlist blue-collar workers and people other than white middle-class folk. Rather than centering on the possibility of a nuclear holocaust—a future death—Jobs with Peace is concerned about the present death and destruction being wrought in this country by the present military buildup. It is not asking for disarmament—just for less waste, no more nuclear weapons, no more programs of foreign military intervention.

The story is told in two parts. First, readers are introduced to an 86-year-old woman who has been a full-time peace activist since August 1945. The action reported is her collecting signatures for a Jobs with Peace petition. The second part is a report on Jobs with Peace activities

For months, at shopping centers and malls, in front of churches and the Co-op, stood a small, white-haired woman in a shawl, her arm cradling a clipboard.

"Are you a registered voter?" she asked in an urgent, unidentifiable accent.

Except it didn't come out that way. She can't quite pronounce "registered" in English. She is Andree Wagner, who was born in Algiers in 1896, received a doctorate in philosophy from the Sorbonne, came to the U.S. to study and teach in 1924. Thirty-seven years ago last Friday, the day an atomic bomb fell on Hiroshima, she became a full-time peace activist.

Because of her accent and determination to work for peace, some people wonder if she's a spy. These people think the U.S. should be "gendarmes of the world," she says.

She is spurred on by a conviction that "When you reach a certain age, you have a duty to the next generation."

Wagner collected signatures "from the early morning until I dropped dead from fatigue."

The Humboldt Jobs with Peace Initiative petition she herself circulated had 6,600 names on it when submitted to the county Election Division last Tuesday. Sixty other people collected about 1,400 more signatures.

To qualify the initiative for the country-wide November ballot, 4,300 of the 8,000 signatures must be validated. The initiative proposes the following: "Shall the People of Humboldt County call upon the U.S. Congress to make more federal funds available for local jobs and vital services in Housing, Health Care, Education, Public Transportation, Public Safety by cutting from the military budget those dollars wasted on military spending unnecessary to our national defense, and redirecting those funds to local jobs serving the people's needs."

The Jobs with Peace Initiative is a nationwide network begun in San Francisco in 1978. After approval there by 61 percent of the voters, similarly-worded initiatives were passed in Madison, Wis., Berkeley, Oakland, Detroit and in five communities in Massachusetts.

Waltham, seat of the military electronics industry in Massachusetts narrowly defeated the measure. Sonoma, Santa Cruz and Humboldt counties were picked by the national network for test campaigns in California this year.

Humboldt was chosen partly because of Wagner's hefty reputation in the peace movement for getting names on petitions. "I am a cog," she says.

And chosen partly because of Humboldt's reputation as a formerly "semi-feudal" county in transformation, with a highly regarded, progressive catalyst in the city of Arcata.

The initiative is not anti-military. "We are not against defense when it is real defense," Wagner says, "but when there is waste."

By diverting those wasted dollars, "All kinds of jobs can be made, in housing, health care and better transportation," Wagner says.

The initiative does make a connection between military spending and high unemployment, between military spending and threatened Social Security cuts.

The university community accepts these ideas, Wagner says, but it is blue collar workers and minorities that the campaign still needs to embrace.

"We try to reach people who are blinded by their problems," she says.

Wagner belongs to many peace organizations. From her perspective, one campaign always leads to the next petition drive. There is no end because there is no peace.

In the coming months, Humboldt Jobs with Peace (JwP) will attempt to document the reasons it gives for proposing the initiative. Namely, that the county has high unemployment; many people here are adversely affected by federal cuts in social programs; work that satisfied people's needs creates more jobs than military ends do; and that military waste exists and is inflationary.

Wagner always carries with her notebooks filled with newsletters and fliers from the peace organizations to which she belongs. JwP is separate from the Nuclear Freeze Initiative, but it has similar goals. Wagner wants you to read this statement: "The money required to provide adequate food, water, education, health and housing for everyone in the world has been estimated at $17 billion a year. It is a huge sum of money...about as much as the world spends on arms every two weeks." She smiles and say to contact her if you ever need to know anything else about peace, because "This is the meaning of my life."

Appeared in the Sunday, August 8, 1982, Times-Standard, Eureka, California. Used here by permission of the newspaper and author. Edited for this publication.

ALL THE WORLD IS LOOKING FOR A SIGN

(Can be sung to the tune: "Who will buy?" from *Oliver!*)

Chorus:
  Who will dare create the new future?
  Who will dare respond to the need?
  All the world looks 'round for a new sign
  The cry for one to risk the deed.

I know that people are responding
Across the villages and towns
They're making claims and new decisions
that turn despair around.

I see men and women working,
Youth and children by their side.
A sense of hope is now emerging,
No way to stop the swelling tide.

I see communities deciding
The future does belong to them.
By corporate effort they are striving
To build the world again.

Final Chorus:
  Who will dare create the new future?
  Who will dare respond to the need?
  All the world looks 'round for a new sign
  So come along with me
  Pick up this destiny
  So come along and build the sign.

Song used by permission of the Institute of Cultural affairs, 4750 North Sheridan Road, Chicago, Illinois, 60640.

JOBS WITH PEACE

by Seth Adler

With activities in more than 150 cities and nearly 100,000 people involved, Jobs with Peace (JwP) Week, April 10-17, 1983, made its impact in more than 35 states. In the city of Philadelphia, one center of activity, organizers had generally the same appraisal. JwP Week broke new ground in linking trade unionists with peace activists, youth with seniors, and victims of budget cuts with civil rights groups. Their common concern was for deep cuts in military spending.

On April 16 in Philadelphia, 65 children marched over a mile in the rain from the School Board to the Federal Building to participate in hearings on local impact of the military budget. They entered the hall with Rep. Bob Edwards, who joined two other congresspersons on the panel. The children testified.

"The children literally took over the hearing," commented John Goldberg of the Philadelphia JwP Campaign. "They filled the room and captivated the audience with accounts of how layoffs were taking their teachers away and how cutbacks had forced them to use a 50-year-old textbook or to sit in a classroom where the paint was peeling and the desks were broken. It was quite moving the way they related these conditions to the threat of nuclear war."

A few days later in Kensington, on the other side of town, another hearing on the military budget took a different turn. Rep. Thomas Foglietta, the only Phildelphia congressperson not to support the JwP congressional resolution, had planned to address a Puerto Rican, Black and white working-class audience. To his surprise, he was silenced before he could begin. JwP participants at the hearing told him not to talk but to listen to what the community had to say.

Some 60 cities saw creative protests of the Pentagon tax on April 15 at post offices and IRS offices. Organizers in Philadelphia took another approach. In a poor section of Germantown, Catholic Bishop Thomas Gumbleton held a JwP rally and conference called "A People's Grand Opening." The bishop and more than 75 neighborhood activities and residents called for the reopening of the boarded-up Acme supermarket. He called the military budget immoral and exhorted the crowd to take a stand against military spending at the expense of poor persons.

In a high school too poor to paint graffiti off the walls, the worldwide escalation of military tensions may seem to be a remote issue. But in West Philly High, a predominantly Black school, these two problems were linked in classes and forums. Every student attended programs on JwP and the military budget, and one popular conclusion was the need for social revolution. Students throughout the Philadelphia school system voted by allocating play money for housing, education, bombs, etc., to indicate the categories for which they would like to see federal taxes spent. Military spending did not fare well.

A JwP labor forum was held at Philadelphia AFSCME District Council 47 headquarters. The event brought out substantial numbers of union members not previously active in political movements. Speaker Thomas Paine Cronin, president of District Council 47, summed up the theme of the forum when he said "corporations, aided by tax breaks, have shipped jobs to low wage countries often dominated by repressive, anti-labor regimes, supported and armed by the U.S. government."

The diversity that marked JwP week activities in Philadelphia was exemplary of what went on elsewhere.

Milwaukee JwP held a five-mile walkathon (the event doubled as a fundraiser) that passed schools, factories and neighborhoods that have fallen victim to the military budget. The event include placing billboards in front of factories, sharing the number of jobs lost.

In Denver, Colorado, the main strategy was to take JwP to the community rather than vice versa. Workshops on the effects of the military budget were held in churches and private homes. Requests for the house meetings far exceeded what the organizers could accommodate. Some meetings attracted up to 40 people.

In Portland, Oregon, people dressed in various occupational uniforms representing the number of jobs created per billion dollars spent. They gathered in the city center to form a "Human Jobs Graph." They showed that spending for the military creates the fewest jobs.

What's up the road for the JwP Campaign? The peace budgets—neighborhood, citywide and now statewide—may make their way to Congress as national legislation. The JwP Budget outlined a program for major job creation, restoration of public services, and the revitalization of transportation, housing and other industries.

These programs would be funded by cuts in the military budget, based on the Congressional Black Caucus Budget Alternative, which includes freezing the nuclear arms race, ending programs designed for foreign intervention, and cutting military waste. JwP referenda are now spreading to cities in Pennsylvania, California, Michigan, West Virginia and New Mexico. They could be used to push Congress to enact JwP legislation.

A referendum instructing congressional representatives to vote for this proposal can be a powerful tool that shows the community just where the representative stands and raises the issue of human needs to a high level of debate throughout the community. Given the current state of the nation, with no signs of abatement in the military budget, unemployment and the worldwide economic crisis, the question of how to force Congress to create massive job programs funded by deep cuts in military spending will become ever more intense. Through concerted organizing for JwP Week the Mobilization for Survival significantly advanced the level of national debate on these issues.

Used by permission of The Mobilizer, Vol. 3—No. 1, Spring 1983, Mobilization for Survival, 853 Broadway, NYC 10003. Edited for this publication.

VICTORY'S CRY

(Can be sung to the tune: "Dakota Hymn")

Beneath the swirl of winds and old worlds,
Still currents stir life's deeps.
Out of the chaos, eyes open wide,
Merge in the silence and beckon new life.
Plunged in night's well, the sun star appears.
Waking the Earth and Sea.

Dancing our dreams and singing our times,
New beings build new lives.
Teamed in the bond of mystery's love,
Transforming souls untouched by hope's trust,
In noontide's heat, communities appear,
Moving the Earth and Sea

Ageless and sweeping as fire through the lands,
New spirit burns new paths.
Soaring as eagles, namelessly rise,
Steadfastly leagued in victory's cry,
Dusk's glory comes as rivers of care
Cover the Earth and Sea.

Song used by permission of the Institute of Cultural Affairs, 4750 North Sheridan Road, Chicago, Illinois, 60640.

TOYS FOR PEACE

by Sue Nichols Spencer

This new, non-profit organization has a four-fold plan of action:

1. *to develop and market a limited number of toys designed to pattern children to pursue peace, not war;*
2. *to urge commercial toy manufacturers to market such toys;*
3. *to furnish manufacturers with ideas and designs for such toys;*
4. *to raise the consciousness of parents about the significance of their toy buying choices and to encourage them to select constructive games and toys.*

Through make-believe and play, children prepare themselves for their futures by acting them out in advance. In environments where nothing is at stake except fun, they try on various roles to test and taste what adult life will be like. In playing house they explore what it will be like to run a household; in racing miniature cars they find out what it will mean to be a motorist; in exchanging play money they get a feeling for buying and selling. The implements they use in playing, their toys are not mere playthings, they are the guide wires of the future.

Toys on the market at the present time are primarily in two categories.

First there are toys with which children are stimulated to act out war and violence. In virtually every store, one finds a plethora of plastic pistols, machine guns, helmets, hand grenades and GI Joes. Then there are the toys with which children may act out the ordinary occupations of life: doctor kits, fire engines, dolls, train sets and building blocks.

However, there are no toys with which children might act out the actual pursuit of peace. Children are furnished the equipment for pretending that they are soldiers but not the equipment for pretending that they are ambassadors. They can be Luke Skywalkers, Great Hulks and Spidermen, but they are not encouraged to be Phillip Habibs, Dag Hammarskjolds or Helen Caldicotts. They can obtain plastic terrains on which to stage mock battles, but they are not offered replicas of the UN's Security Council room with which to practice arguing conflicts to a peaceful solution.

War toys make our children highly conscious of military careers and endeavors. They serve to eclipse those diplomatic efforts upon which the children's futures actually and truly hang. War toys discourage the development of verbal skills. They foster in children the belief that the acceptable way to settle conflicts is the quick, easy one of eliminating the protagonist. Violence is seen as the first, rather than the last, resort.

By offering no countering toys for playing the pursuit of peace, we imply that such activities are beyond the purview of ordinary people and must be handled by another echelon of beings. Of course the terrible truth is that the pursuit must become increasingly the concern of everyone.

We need toys for peace. And the Toys for Peace organization needs moral and financial support as well as artistic and design talent. For further information about how you can help write: Toys for Peace, Sue Spencer—President, 205 E. Leeland Heights Blvd., Lehigh Acres, FL 33936. Phone: (813) 369-6650

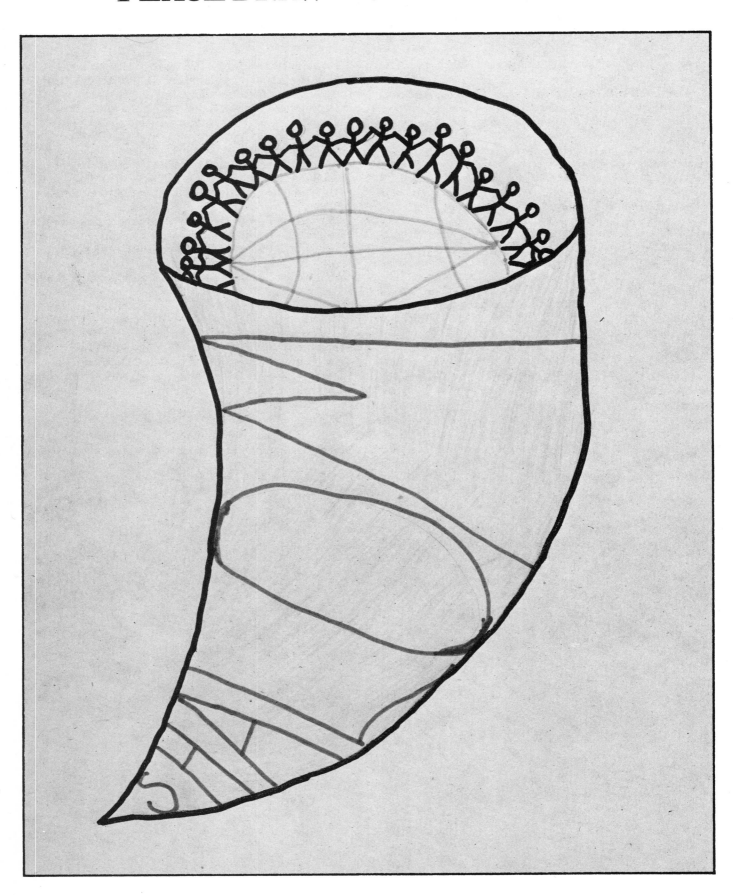

PEACE

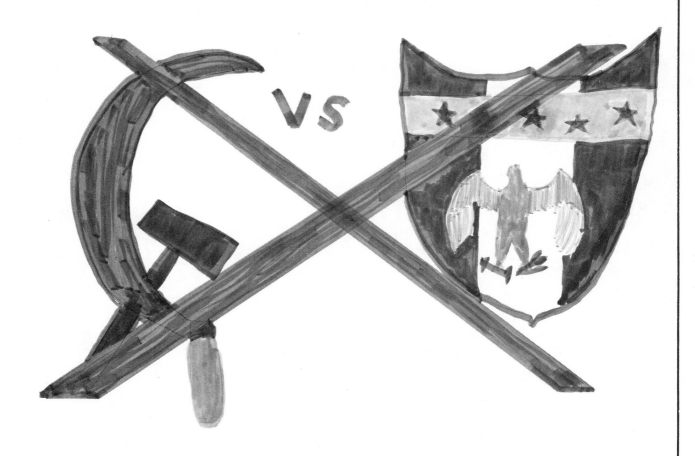

VS

Peace

Around the World

MAKE PEACE
MAKE FRIENDS

BIBLIOGRAPHIES
Compiled by Connie Johnson, author of *Living Our Visions of Peace*

BIBLIOGRAPHY OF AUDIO VISUAL AIDS AND SOURCES

The Big If: 16mm sound film; color; 9 minutes; rental $25, Journal films. This animated film produced by the United Nations envisions what the world would be like if armaments were transformed into implements of peace.

Bombs Will Make the Rainbow Break: 16mm sound film and videocassette; color; 17 minutes; rental $45, Films Incorporated. This intense, inspiring film dramatizes through the innocence of children's artwork and the simplicity of their works the impact of growing up in a world on the brink of nuclear destruction. Grade school children in New York tell how the constant threat of nuclear war is affecting their lives.

Every Heart Beats True: film strip or slide format; 140 frames; 25 minutes; audiocassette. Sale $24 filmstrip, $53 slides, Packard Manse Media Project. The presentation is addressed to youth who must decide whether to march in step to the beat of war or to follow Christian convictions about being peacemakers.

Gods of Metal: 16mm sound film; color; 27 minutes; rental $25, Maryknoll Films. The arms race is analyzed from a Christian perspective showing the economic and social effects on people in the United States and throughout the world. Emphasizes the necessity for individual responsibility to halt the arms build-up.

Hear Peace Here: sound recording; 30 minutes; 33-1/3 rpm record; sale $5.95, Friendship Press. The record contains discussion provoking, dramatized vignettes on peace issues.

If You Love This Planet: 16mm sound film; color; 26 minutes; rental $30, National Film Board of Canada. This award-winning documentary featuring Dr. Helen Caldicott, national president of Physicians for Social Responsibility, looks at what our planet might be like in the aftermath of a nuclear war.

In The Nuclear Shadow: 16mm sound film; color; 25 minutes; rental $46, Educational Film and Video Project. Subtitled "What Can the Children Tell Us," this documentary features children of various ages, races and backgrounds sharing their feelings about the arms race and the possibility of a nuclear holocaust.

The Last Epidemic: 16mm sound film and videocassette formats; color; 36 minutes; rental $50, Resource Center for Nonviolence. At a conference of Physicians for Social Responsibility, speakers describe what would happen if a one-megaton nuclear bomb were to be detonated over downtown San Francisco.

The Magician: 16mm sound film; black and white; 13 minutes; rental $40, Films Incorporated. This stark parable of a magician on a lonely beach who beguiles a group of children into his shooting gallery is a biting commentary on the horrors of militarism and war.

The Peace Movement in Europe: 3/4 inch videocassette; 30 minutes; rental $15, EcuFILM. Pierre Salinger talks in Paris with three leading figures in the European Peace Movement about their goals, involvement of church groups, hopes for disarmament and other means toward peace.

Peace: A Conscious Choice: 16mm sound film; color; 4 minutes; rental $20, Bullfrog Films. Striking visuals and powerful music are combined to resolve the "Us vs. Them" standoff and move to personal action for peace in the spirit of Ghandi.

Top Priority: 16mm sound film; color; 9 minutes; rental $40, Encyclopedia Britannica. This animated film poses the question: What's more important, water or missiles?

War Without Winners: 16mm sound film; color; 28 minutes; rental $50, Films Incorporated. Produced by the Center for Defense Information, this film examines such issues as the power of nuclear weapons, the complexities of the arms race and the implications of the SALT treaties.

NOTE: Many of these titles are available from your regional or denominational media/film libraries, often at a lower cost. Check there first. Also, Films Incorporated has developed a collection of "Films on War and Peace in the Nuclear Age" — with several films and videotapes included. Write for a brochure describing this collection.

Very helpful resource for intensive, intentional use. Addresses of distributors:

Bullfrog Films, Inc., Oley, PA 19457 (215) 779-8226

EcuFILM, 810 Twelfth Ave., South Nashville, TN 37203 (800) 251-4091 (615) 242-6277

Educational Film and Video Project, 1725B Seabright Ave., Santa Cruz, CA 95062 (408) 427-2627

Encyclopedia Britannica Education Corporation, 425 North Michigan Ave., Chicago, IL 60611 (800) 621-3900

Films Incorporated, 1213 Wilmette Ave., Wilmette, IL 60091 (800) 323-4222

Friendship Press, 475 Riverside Drive, New York, NY 10115 (212) 870-2495

Journal Films, 930 Pitner Ave., Evanston, IL 60202 (312) 328-6700

Maryknoll Films, Maryknoll, NY 10545

National Film Board of Canada, U.S. Distributor: Direct Cinema Ltd., Box 69589, Los Angeles, CA 90069

Canadian users contact local National Film Board of Canada outlet.

Packard Manse Media Project, P.O. Box 450, Stoughton, MA 02072

Resource Center for Nonviolence, P.O. Box 2324, Santa Cruz, CA 95063 (408) 423-1626

BIBLIOGRAPHY OF BOOKS FOR CHILDREN AND YOUTH

A Boat to Nowhere, Maureen Crane Wartski, Westminster, 1980. This story of Vietnamese boat people is for older readers. It contains the account of difficult times at sea and rejection at landing. Difficult but true account.

A Toad for Tuesday, Russell E. Erickson, Lothrop, 1974. This young child's book illustrates how offering friendship to an enemy can make them into a friend. The characters are a toad and an owl.

The Bronze Bow, Elizabeth Speare, Houghton Mifflin, 1961. Historical fiction for older readers that chronicles a young man's fight against the Roman legions. The story follows his change from hate to an attitude of love and acceptance.

Coals of Fire, Elizabeth H. Bauman, Herald Press, 1954. This collection of stories tell of people who lived out their love for both friends and enemies and accepted the consequences.

Cross-Fire: A Vietnam Novel, Gail B. Graham, Pantheon Books, 1972. A tragic story for older readers that details the wastefulness of war. It holds the old theme that fear turns men into beasts.

Days of Terror, Barbara Smucker, Herald Press, 1979. This story of a Russian family's emigration to Canada to escape the Revolution lifts up a peace theme. Older readers will find this story holds their attention.

The Diddakoi, Rumer Godden, Viking, 1972. A story about a seven year old gypsy who is not accepted until performing a herioc rescue during a fire. For juniors.

The Elephant Who Couldn't Forget, Faith McNulty, Harper & Row, 1980. Grandmother helps her young grandson to learn that he needs to remember what is important and forget what is unimportant. In this case, forget the unkind treatment of his brother.

Fly Away Home, Christine Nostlinger, translated from German by Anthea Bell, Franklin Watts Inc., 1975. This is the story of the survival of a family during war. The eight year old girl expresses her fears and demonstrates her maturation.

The Friendly Story Caravan, Anna Pettit Broomell, Pendle Hill, 1981. The book includes thirty-one stories of Christian living. The ethical principles include non-violence.

The Happy Owls, Celestino Piatti, Atheneum, 1964. This story relates the owls secret for being happy and living in peace. The questioners don't understand the secret. For preschoolers.

The Hating Book, Charlotte Shapiro Zolotow, Harper, 1966. This story illustrates the results of gossip and hate.

Henry's Red Sea, Barbara Smucker, Herald Press, 1955. This action filled story of Polish and Russian Mennonites following World War I is for Juniors.

Herbie's Troubles, Carol Chapman, E.P. Dutton, 1981. A first grader tries to handle a troublemaker. After securing his friends' advice he devises his own peaceful solution. Good for primaries.

How the Children Stopped the Wars, Jan Wahl, Avon, 1972. A shepherd boy leads hundreds of children in a successful effort to stop the wars that took their fathers away from home.

The Hunter and the Animals — A Wordless Picture Book, Tomie de Paola, Holiday House, 1981. This preschool book can be "read" by children or adults to describe the hunter's eventual reconciliation.

I Am Fifteen and I Don't Want to Die, Christine Arnothy, E.P. Dutton, 1956. The book tells the story of a fifteen year old Hungarian who lives through the Nazi defense of Budapest. The story of the shortages, the deaths and eventual escape detail the plight of civilians in wartime.

I'm Really Dragged But Nothing Gets Me Down, Nat Hentoff, Simon and Schuster, 1968. This father-son conflict leaves the solutions open ended but provides some values and choices leading to the alternatives in becoming a draft resistor. For youth.

In Search of Peace, Roberta Strauss Feuerlicht, Julian Messner, 1970. Stories of the four Americans who had won the Nobel Peace Prize at that time: Theodore Roosevelt, Jane Addams, Ralph Bunche and Martin Luther King, Jr.

Jenny Learns a Lesson, Gyo Fujikawa, Grosset & Dunlap, 1980. This story for young children describes the pretend play of a young girl who learns to plan fun that does not center around herself.

Joining the Army that Sheds No Blood, Susan Clemmer Steiner, Herald Press, 1982. Serious book that covers war, peace, duty to government, responsibility to God and peace within and with others. Youth will also appreciate the pointed cartoons.

The Journey Back, Johanna Russ, Thomas Y. Crowell Company, 1976. This is the story of a young Jewish girl trying to rebuild her life after war. A story of family problems that takes place in Holland. For youth.

Journey Home, Yoshiko Uchida, Atheneum, 1978. Sequel to:

Journey to Topaz in which a Japanese-American on the West Coast loses home and must spend years rebuilding life. Help comes from an American neighbor.

The Last Knife, Annabel Jones Johnson and Edgar Raymond Johnson, Simon and Schuster, 1971. This story is for youth. It details the shame of a younger brother for his older brother who is in jail because of his conscientious objector stand. Insight about the situation comes from six stories about others who have chosen conscientious objector status.

Let's Be Enemies, Janice May Udry, Harper, 1961. Two young children learn that hating your friend leads to being lonesome, but sharing is friendship. Excellent identification for boys and girls.

The Little Brute Family, Russell Hoban, Avon Camelot, 1980. Young children will love and learn from this story of a family that learns to care for each other and indicate the change by taking a new name, "Nice."

The Little Fishes, Erik Christian Haugaard, Houghton Mifflin, 1978. Juniors will find this story of three children on their own in Italy during World War II challenging as it clearly shares the horrors of war but also shares understanding and love.

Loaves and Fishes, Linda Hunt, Marianne Frase and Doris Liebert, Herald Press, 1980. A cookbook for young children that introduces the concept that peace is more likely to exist where everyone has enough to eat. The book balances world hunger with thoughtful use of our own resources.

My Enemy, My Brother, James Forman, Scholastic Book Service, 1972. This story of a 16 year old pacifist who survives a concentration camp with his grandfather describes his intellectual journey when he is forced to act contrary to his convictions. Heavy going for juniors and older.

My Friend the Monster, Robert Bulla, Crowell, 1980. This story illustrates the benefits that come from making friends with someone who is different. Fairy tale for children.

The Path of Most Resistance, Melissa Miller and Phil M. Shenk, Herald Press, 1982. The collection of ten stories of young men who resisted the draft during the Vietnam War present challenging reading for young people and older ones, too. (Mennonite young persons)

Peace Be With You, Cornelia Lehn, Faith and Life Press, 1981. A collection of fifty-nine stories of persons who have believed in living out their peace convictions. Suitable for all ages.

Peace Is An Adventure, Emery Kelen, Meredith Press, 1967. This book describes the work of people of the United Nations working for peace around the world.

The Pinkish, Purplish, Bluish Egg, Bill Peet, Houghton Mifflin, Co., 1963. A dove hatches an egg that becomes a 1/2 lion and 1/2 eagle that is too strange to be accepted until he finds a peaceful solution to a menacing problem. Children will love it.

People, Peter Spier, Doubleday, 1980. Picture book or storybook, either use carries the same message: people are different in wonderful ways and should be appreciated, not hated, for the diversity. Everyone will want to glance through.

Peter's Chair, Ezra Jack Keats, Harper & Row, 1967. This classic children's book handles the sibling rivalry that happens when the second child appears. Healthy model for working through angry feelings.

The Quarreling Book, Charlotte Zolotow, Harper & Row, 1963. Clever tale for children that illustrates the chain reaction of the sharp response. The family dog reverses the chain in this story. Added touch is the parent's kiss. Nice.

Sadako and the Thousand Paper Cranes, Eleanor Coerr, Dell Yearling, 1980. The biography of Sadako and her death from leukemia as a result of the Hiroshima bombing is a powerful word for peace. This is written for young children.

The Singing Tree, Kate Seredy, Viking Press, 1967. Family life set in Hungary during World War II illustrates the far reaching effects of war and the difficulty children have in understanding hate that is great enough to cause war. For juniors.

The Story of Ferdinand, Munro Leaf, Puffin, 1977. A preschool classic about the bull that was chosen for the bull fights but loves peace. The happy ending pleases all.

Study War No More: a Peace Handbook for Youth, edited by David S. Young, Brethren Press, 1981. Studybook includes stories of peacemakers, suggested activities, games and discussion questions for junior and senior high's.

Surviving Fights With Your Brothers and Sisters, Joy Wilt, Word, 1979. Excellent choice for juniors that helps them identify causes for family fights and positive ways to handle the problem, bringing peace. Read to younger children.

The Tomato Patch, William Wondriska, Holt, Rinehart and Winston, Inc., 1964. The tale of two kingdoms that have spent all their time preparing for war and have forgotten how to grow food, weave, etc. Two young princes meet in the separating forrest and learn to grow tomatoes which leads to peaceful co-existence.

Two Sides of the River, David Crippen, Abingdon, 1976. Two families separated by a river are enemies in a third generation feud. The tale of their making peace is exciting.

Underground to Canada, Barbara Smucker, Clark-Irwin, 1977. Two young slave girls escape from a Mississippi plantation and travel the underground railway to Canada. Human dignity, kindness and bravery prevail. Juniors will read this with interest.

Wacky and His Fuddlejig, Stanford Summers, Stanford Summers, 1980. Christmas story of Santa's helper who was so upset by toy guns and tanks that he creates his own new toy, the fuddlejig. The story describes how it becomes the favorite toy of children. A story for young children.

The Wind is Not a River, Arnold Alfred Griese, Thomas Y. Crowell Company, Inc., 1978. A story for juniors from World War II in the Aleutian Islands. Two children rescue a Japanese soldier and are caught in the values conflict between old ways and the new.

BIBLIOGRAPHY FOR PARENTS AND TEACHER/LEADERS

A Manual on Nonviolence and Children, Stephanie Judson, Friends Peace Committee, 1977.

A Teacher's Resource Manual on Multi-Ethnicity and Global Awareness, Alexander R. Korff, Justice and Peace Center.

Building Blocks for Peace, Margaret Comstock, the Jane Addams Peace Association.

Doing the Word: A Manual for Christian Education Shared Approaches, Georgeann Wilcoxson, United Church Press, 1977.

Family Adventures Toward Shalom, Ecumenical Task Force on Christian Education for World Peace, 1979.

Global Dimensions in U.S. Education: The Elementary School, Judith V. Torney and Donald N. Morris, Center for War/Peace Studies, 1972.

How to Teach Peace to Children, J. Lorne Peachey, Herald Press, 1981.

Morality of Power: A Notebook on Christian Education for Social Change, Charles R. McCollough, United Church Press, 1977.

Parenting for Peace and Justice, Kathleen and James McGinnis, Orbis Books, 1981.

Peace Education Age-Level Guidelines, Tricia de Beer et al., Shalom Education.

Peace Is Possible: A Study/Action Process Guide on Peacemaking, Shirley J. Heckman, United Church Press, 1982.

Peacemaking and the Community of Faith: A Handbook for Congregations, John A. Donaghy, fellowship of Reconciliation, 1982.

Peacemaking: Family Activities for Justice and Peace, Jacqueline Haessly, Paulist Press, 1980.

Values Clarification: A Handbook of Practical Strategies for Teachers and Students, Sidney B. Simon, Leland W. Howe and Howard Kirschenbaum, Hart Publishing Company, Inc., 1979.

Why People Fight: Teacher's Book, James E. Boler, United Church Press, 1975.

Why People Fight: Student Project Book, James E. Boler, Unitec Church Press, 1975.

PHILOSOPHY OF EDUCATION FOR MISSION

Mission is at the heart and center of the Church's life; through the centuries, people of faith have witnessed in word and in deed everywhere on earth. To be the church is to be in mission.

Education for mission enables people to discover the meaning of mission; to learn about the church's involvement throughout the world; to prepare themselves for ministry in mission; and to engage individually and corporately in expressions of mission. Education for mission can be defined as equipping the people of God so that they may widen their vision and invest their strength in meeting opportunities for mission now before them.

MISSION

Mission is obedient response to our Lord and Saviour. The risen Christ commissioned his followers to witness to God's love for the world through word and deed. This commission cannot be understood apart from the story of God's action in the world which we find in the scriptures of the Old and New Testaments where we hear the call to live in trust and partnership with God and to participate in the fulfillment of God's purposes in history.

EDUCATION FOR MISSION

Education for mission is necessary because of the tension, incongruity and contradiction which individual Christians and local congregations experience between the gospel proclaimed and the realities of life in the world. Inappropriate ways of dealing with that tension are: to conform; to condemn; to retreat. For people of faith, the only acceptable relationship between the gospel and the world is to live in the midst of the world as ambassadors for Christ: to love the world as God loves it; to serve in the world in such a way as to witness to God's love.

FOR

The middle word of 'education for mission' implies intention and sets the direction. The task is not only to educate *about* mission but to educate toward the clear goal of active participation in God's cause as it is revealed to us in Jesus Christ.

EDUCATION

It is the nature of the community of faith to nurture its members so that they will grow in faith and develop the strength to confront the conflicting experiences of life both within the community and beyond it.

Education sometimes takes place in an individual's encounter with a committed person. It is often a group experience. It always involves relationships—within one's self, between individuals, among people. Thus the leadership style of intentional educational experiences is one of interaction with the participants—teacher and learners being partners in learning.

Education can help people and groups overcome limiting ways and move into more mature expressions of faith. Learning can be said to have taken place when learners are living what they say they believe.

Education is not neutral. It either helps to maintain what is or it enables people to anticipate and live toward new futures for themselves and the world. The latter requires an educational process which integrates awareness, analysis, action and reflection based on the assumption that we learn as we are involved.

March 1983